The ABC's of Novell® NetWare®

Jeff Woodward

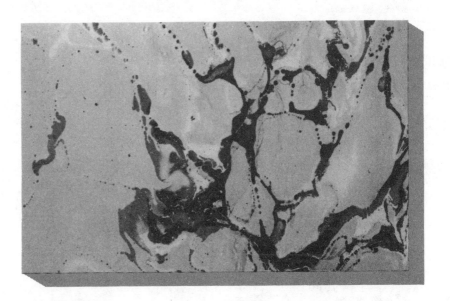

SYBEX®

San Francisco/Paris/Düsseldorf/London

Acquisitions Editor: Dianne King
Developmental Editor: Cheryl Holzaepfel
Copy Editor: Alan Hislop
Technical Editors: Carlo Cupini and Steve Nitenson
Word Processor: Deborah Maizels
Book Designer: Jeffrey James Giese
Chapter Art: Eleanor Ramos
Technical Art: Jeffrey James Giese
Screen Graphics: Sonja Schenk
Typesetter: The Typesetting Shop, Inc.
Proofreader: Edith Rex
Indexer: Ted Laux
Cover Designer: Thomas Ingalls + Associates
Cover Photographer: Mark Johann

Acknowledgments

Writing is often spoken of as a lonely, solitary profession—an individual battling mightily to fashion concepts, thoughts, ideas, and words into a written form that, hopefully, brings enlightenment to others. Being a writer, I know that this is true, but only to a certain extent. There are countless individuals who labor vigorously to make a book such as *The ABC's of Novell NetWare* a living reality. Many of these people the writer never sees or meets, but they are there, sharing the same frustrations and satisfactions as they mold the writer's creation into existence. So, the way I see it, I'm never alone.

The ABC's of Novell NetWare reflects the synthetic efforts of a great many people at SYBEX, unknown to me, but greatly appreciated for their creative input and hard work.

There are several people I want to thank specifically for their support of this project:

Cheryl Holzaepfel, my editor, for her patience, support, good humor, and untiring efforts that kept me organized and on the right track. She is a writer's delight.

Dianne King, for thinking of me for this project. When I needed assistance, she cheerfully made things happen when no one else could.

Hannah Robinson, for her positive encouragement, without which I would never have considered writing this book.

Dr. Rudy Langer, for giving the go-ahead to this much needed project.

Steve Nitenson, Information Systems Analyst at Kaiser Permanente Medical Center, South San Francisco, whose tremendous enthusiasm propelled this project into being.

I want to thank Novell for developing the NetWare program, which has transformed countless business organizations into paragons of efficiency. There are several people at Novell to whom I want to send a special thanks:

To Carlo Cupini, a Novell NetWare genius, who was there every step of the way, from the first meeting in Provo, Utah to the final technical editing. He was always generous with his time and his support, and I am most grateful.

To Becky Poulter, for providing me with the voluminous NetWare documentation and the computer-based training software.

To Patty Heiser, for informing me of the day-to-day progress of the status of the file server. When I thought things would never happen, her cheerful voice was there to reassure me.

And last, but certainly not least, to Diane Woodward, my loving wife, without whose support I would not have had the time to devote to this project.

Jeff Woodward
Los Angeles, California
4 July 1989

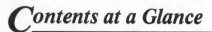

Contents at a Glance

*T*able of Contents

Introduction

Why a book about Novell NetWare? Because it is very much needed. Though the NetWare program comes with a voluminous set of documentation, most of it deals with the installation of the system and the network supervisor's responsibilities. True, some of this documentation is for Novell users, but it is usually kept in the care of the supervisor, or at best, is located where users must leave their desks in order to refer to it. This is inconvenient and impractical, especially for beginners. Unless you are fortunate to have a supervisor who is willing to write out network operating instructions for each user, you will find it difficult to work on the network.

That's where this book comes in—*The ABC's of Novell NetWare* provides you with all the information necessary to get up and running on the network quickly and easily. Everything you need to know to get started is in this one book. For those of you who are new to computers, you'll find basic information about personal computers. The book also includes introductions to three popular data processing programs: WordPerfect 5, Lotus 1-2-3, and dBASE IV.

Who Is This Book For?

Exploring the world of computing can be exciting and rewarding, but it can involve a certain amount of intimidation and confusion. A new computer user is like an inexperienced traveler discovering new and fascinating lands, but also having to overcome many unknown obstacles along the way.

Any experienced traveler knows that a good map and guide book are indispensable aids to navigating around an unfamiliar country. *The ABC's of Novell NetWare* is your map and guide book through the world of computing on the Novell NetWare network. This book is specifically designed for those of you who are new to computers, new to working on a Novell NetWare network, or new to any of three popular data processing programs—WordPerfect 5, Lotus 1-2-3, and dBASE IV. If you are an experienced Novell network user, but have never had the chance to explore the potential of what NetWare offers, you will find this book very helpful in expanding your skills.

How Is This Book Organized?

This book has three parts. Each is a small world of its own, yet each part shares aspects with the others.

Part I consists of Chapters 1-4 and familiarizes you with your personal computer and the Novell networking system.

Chapter 1 introduces you to the physical components of the computer system. Knowing about the equipment you work with makes it easier to do your job. You'll also learn about the various types of programs you may be using to perform your business tasks.

Chapter 2 discusses the importance of computer memory. If you're a newcomer to computers, this chapter is a must. Without memory, there is no computing.

Chapter 3 teaches you how to use DOS, the disk operating system, to organize a file storage and management system. You'll learn how to start your computer, work with directories, format floppy disks, make backup copies of important data, and work with files.

Chapter 4 is an overview of the Novell NetWare network environment. It describes the physical components that make up the network and how they are used. You'll find out who works on a network and what their individual responsibilities are. You will also be introduced to the concepts of network security and organization.

Part II, Chapters 5-8, shows you how to use the NetWare operating system. Novell NetWare has a totally different system from DOS, the operating system that runs your personal computer, yet it works hand in hand with DOS. You will see how closely related these two systems are as you work your way through the book.

Chapter 5 introduces you to the mechanics of working on the network. You'll learn how to log in, see who else is assigned as a network user, and send messages to users currently using the network. You'll also learn about the security procedures for entering the network.

Chapter 6 shows you how to organize and manage network directories, which are areas on the computer designated for storing your files. You'll perform exercises to create, move between, rename, and delete these directories.

Chapter 7 provides hands-on exercises that guide you through file management procedures such as renaming, copying, and deleting files. You'll also learn about file security.

Chapter 8 guides you through the basics of printing on the network. Printing on the network can be a very confusing process, more so than any other aspect of working on a network, so I recommend you read this chapter thoroughly.

Part III, Chapters 9-11, presents three popular data processing programs commonly used on networks. These chapters cover the basic procedures needed to get you started on each program.

Chapter 9 introduces you to WordPerfect 5, one of the most powerful word processors on the market today. You will learn how to start the program, create and edit a sample document, print it, and save it.

Chapter 10 gives you a basic introduction to the powers of Lotus 1-2-3. If number crunching is your business, this program is the one for you. In this chapter you will learn how to create a small spreadsheet and perform some basic calculations.

Chapter 11 discusses the rudiments of dBASE IV, a powerful database management program. You'll build a database structure, fill it with information, and do some simple editing.

The Appendix provides useful information that supplements the main text. It shows you how to create or modify your network login script, a set of instructions that the network operating system performs when you enter the network.

How to Use This Book

The ABC's of Novell is primarily a tutorial, providing useful, hands-on exercises that reinforce the information you read about. Learning how to use your computer on the NetWare network is easier when you actually work with the material and see the results. Each exercise has step-by-step numbered instructions that require you to type in information or commands. Text that you are to type appears in bold letters or characters and is presented in two ways. One way looks similar to this:

2. At the DOS prompt, type

   PROMPT PG

   and press the Enter key.

The second way is similar to this:

4. At the DOS prompt, type **MAP** and press the Enter key.

In most instances, the examples given in the exercises in this book should be typed in exactly as you see them. There are occasions, however, when an italicized generic example of an entry is given. For example, you may see an instruction like this:

3. At the DOS prompt, type

drive letter:\directory name\file name

In this case, you would substitute an actual drive letter, directory name, and file name for the italicized ones. For instance, you might type

C:\REPORTS\JONES.LTR

You will also be able to use this book as a reference when you need to refer back to information you have learned. The index will give you the page number of a particular item of interest. Inside the covers of this book you will find useful reference information concerning the different utilities found in NetWare and the tasks they perform. You will also find a guide to the options used with a few of the most used NetWare printing commands.

If you are experienced with personal computers and feel you have a good understanding of your computer system and how DOS works, you may want to skip Chapters 1-3 and immediately begin with Chapter 4, *An Introduction to Novell NetWare.* If you are a new user and need to get started on the network immediately, you can go directly to Chapter 5, *Entering the Network.* Then, when you have time, go back up and read Part I.

You now should be ready to start on your journey through the world of NetWare, with *The ABC's of Novell NetWare* as your personal guide book. I hope it is helpful and you find your experience with NetWare pleasant and useful.

NOVELL NETWARE

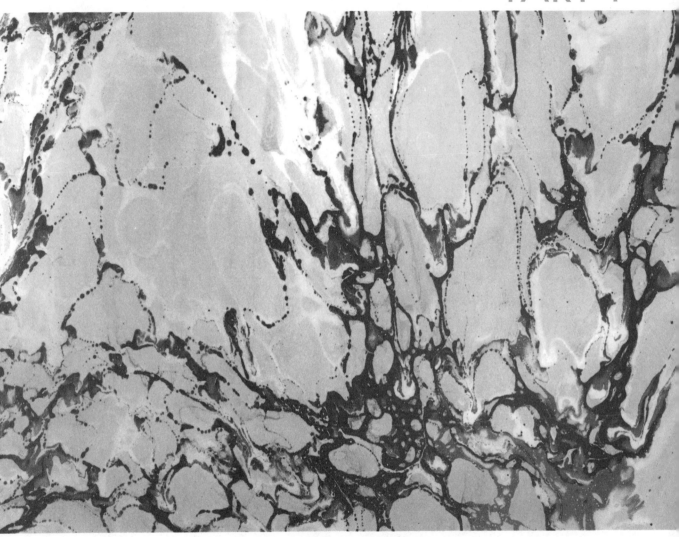

PART 1

Getting Acquainted with Novell and Your Computer

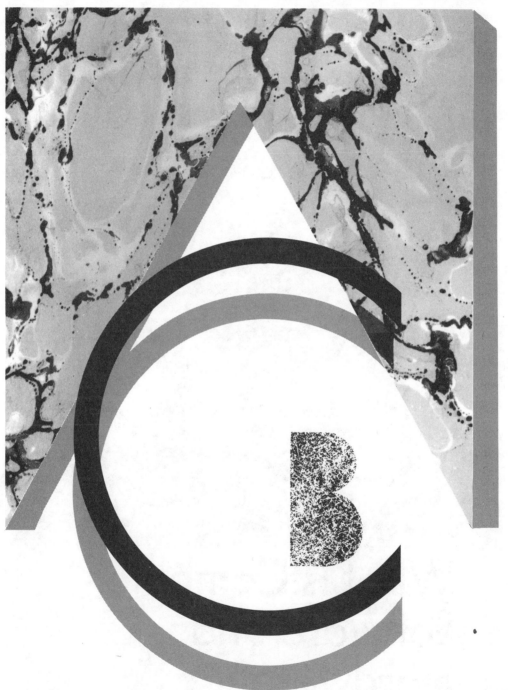

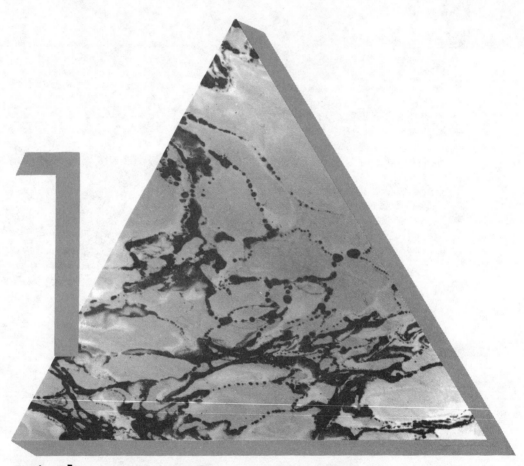

What Is Computer Software and Hardware?

The physical components that make up a computer system are known as computer hardware. This equipment is needed to operate the software programs that allow you to do your job, whether that job be word processing, payroll and accounting, graphics, creating spreadsheets, desktop publishing, or managing databases.

A n Introduction to Computer Hardware

The main hardware components of most computer systems are the central processing unit, the monitor, the keyboard, the printer, hard- and floppy-disk drives, and, in some cases, a mouse (not of the furry variety). A basic knowledge of these items will allow you to use your system more efficiently.

T he CPU

CPU stands for *central processing unit* or, in simpler terms, the actual computer. Computers come in different shapes and sizes, depending on the make and model of the system. They all do the same thing, however: they make it easier and faster for you to get your job done well and efficiently.

Built into the CPU are tiny *microchips*, or more simply *chips,* that process and store the information entered into the system. These chips are complex electrical conduits that organize and move vast amounts of electronic information at incredible speeds between keyboard, disk drives, monitor, and printer. Chips are the workhorses of the system. Without them there would be no desktop computers, and you would probably still be using a typewriter. Sometimes it is helpful to think of the CPU as a powerful factory, designed to process and distribute information between the pieces of equipment connected to it.

Figure 1.1 depicts the hardware components that make up most computer systems.

D isks and Disk Drives

Most of you work with computers that have at least one of the following disk drives—floppy-disk drives (5¼ or 3½ inches in diameter) and hard-disk drives. Some CPUs are set up without disk drives,

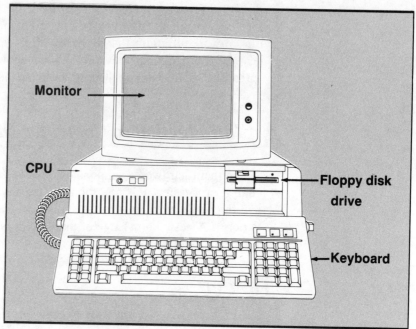

Figure 1.1: *The personal computer*

so don't be surprised if you don't have one. These computers are known as *diskless workstations* and are used with networks. If you have a diskless workstation, you can run software applications and retrieve data files stored on a central computer, but without a floppy-disk drive you will not be able to install new software programs.

Hard Disks and Hard-Disk Drives

The *hard-disk drive* is inside the CPU and consists of several hard, data-storage disks, stacked on top of one another, that electronically record information created at the keyboard. Hard disks have two key advantages over floppy disks: they can store very large amounts of data, and the transfer of data between the hard disk and the CPU is very rapid. (The sound of an active hard-disk drive may remind you of a tiny woodpecker, quietly tapping away inside your computer.)

Floppy Disks and Floppy-Disk Drives

Floppy-disk drives are on the front of the computer. The drive consists primarily of a motor that turns a plastic disk, and electronic heads that read and write data directly onto the disk. These plastic disks, which you insert manually, are termed *floppy disks* because they are flexible. They perform the same storage function as the hard disk. Compared to a hard disk, however, they are limited in the amount of available data-storage space and are much slower in transferring information between the microchips and the disk.

Each of the several types of floppy disks provides a different amount of storage space. For example, you can store approximately 250 pages of double-spaced text on a 360-kilobyte (K), double-density disk. (One kilobyte equals approximately 1,000 bytes; one byte of data corresponds to one character of text.)

Disk Type	Storage Space
5¼-inch double-density	360 K (360,000 bytes)
5¼-inch high-density	1.2 megabytes (1,200,000 bytes)
3½-inch double-density	720 K (720,000 bytes)
3½-inch high-density	1.44 megabytes (1,400,000 bytes)

If you have a double-density disk drive, you cannot use high-density disks in it. However, you can use a double-density disk in a high-density drive. If you aren't sure which type of drive you have in your computer, ask your supervisor.

Handling Floppy Disks

The work you do on your computer will probably be stored on a hard disk, where it is more easily accessible than on a floppy disk. If you are wise, however, you will make a duplicate copy of your work on a floppy disk. It is important to adhere to a few rules when handling your floppy disks in order to prevent the loss of valuable information:

- Never touch the exposed areas of a disk. You can see the surface of the disk through three openings in the disk cover (see Figure 1.2). The long oval slot is where the computer physically reads and writes data. Oils from your skin can damage these sensitive plastic surfaces.

- Never place disks near magnetized objects. Electromagnetic energy can alter the electronically coded data on the disk.

- Never place disks in areas that undergo extreme changes in temperature. Try to store your disks in a location that is always at room temperature.

- Never place disks near any solvent or liquid that gives off corrosive vapors, such as glues or thinners. These vapors can eat into the plastic disk.

- Never write on a disk label with a pencil or ball point pen after the label is mounted on the disk. Too much pressure can damage the surface of the disk.

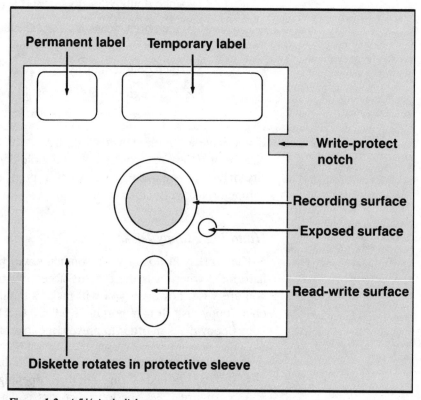

Figure 1.2: A 5¼-inch diskette

Protecting Data Stored on a Disk

It is important to protect information from being accidentally erased or written over by new information when you want only to read the information on a disk and not edit it. Each box of new disks comes with a sheet of small, rectangular gummed tabs, often silver or black in color. These tabs are called *write-protect tabs*. To protect your data on a 5¼-inch disk, place one of these tabs over the write-protect notch (see Figure 1.2). Peel the write-protect tab off the notch when you want to record new information or erase current information stored on the disk.

A 3½-inch disk comes with a write-protect tab built into the casing that surrounds the disk. The write-protect notch is the small square window with the tab that can be moved back and forth (see Figure 1.3). To write-protect this disk, slide the tab in the direction that allows you to see through the hole that the tab covers. Close this hole if you want to write data to the disk.

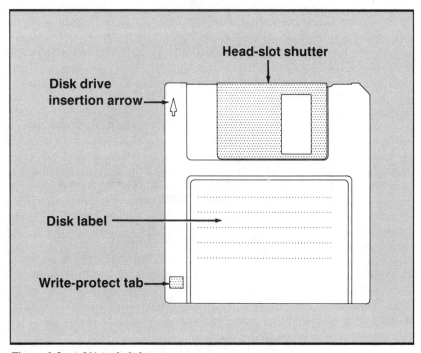

Figure 1.3: A 3½-inch diskette

Inserting a Disk into a Floppy-Disk Drive

Placing a disk in a floppy-disk drive is easy to do. You may at some point, however, accidently insert a disk sideways or backward, especially if you place your computer on its side under the desk in order to have more desktop working space. The results of incorrectly inserting a disk aren't disastrous, but doing so can be confusing and can cause a little anxiety until the problem is corrected.

Obtain a floppy disk and follow these steps:

1. Remove the disk from its protective sleeve by placing your thumb on the label and your remaining fingers underneath the disk. As you pull the disk free, the oval slot should be facing away from your thumb. Be careful not to touch the exposed surface of the disk.

2. If it is not already open, open the drive latch that covers the slot in the disk drive.

3. With the label side up, or facing the top surface of the computer, gently slide the disk into the slot, being careful not to bend it.

4. Close the drive latch. Closing the latch lowers the drive heads into the proper position for reading and writing on the disk.

If you incorrectly place a floppy disk into a disk drive and try to access the disk, you will receive the following message on your monitor screen:

Not ready error reading drive A
Abort, Retry, Fail?

If this message appears, check to see if the disk is inserted in the proper direction. If the red light on the disk drive is on, wait until it goes out before removing the disk. After you correct the placement of the disk, press the A key to abort the operation so you will be able to read the disk.

*T*he Monitor

The monitor is the television-like screen on which you view your documents. Although it may look like a television set, it does not operate like one. Like CPUs, monitors vary in shape and size, and their quality of resolution also varies. Most businesses provide monochrome monitors because they are less expensive than color. Monochrome monitors usually display information in either green or amber on a black background. Most people find the amber color less fatiguing to the eye when stared at for long periods of time.

If you are fortunate enough to have a color monitor, you can take advantage of the customizing color options provided by most software applications. Finding a color scheme that works best for you can reduce fatigue and add interest to your monitor screen.

*T*he Keyboard

The computer keyboard is similar to the conventional typewriter keyboard, with some major differences. For example, the computer keyboard has special keys that, when used alone or in combination with other keys, perform special functions that are determined by the software program you are operating. A description of how they're used will be found in the documentation for that particular program. A computer keyboard also has a separate numeric pad to assist you when you are working with programs that require extensive numerical input.

Figure 1.4 shows you the three most common keyboards. Each one has a different arrangement of keys, but don't let this confuse you; they all accomplish the same tasks. For purposes of discussion in this book, I will assume you have an enhanced keyboard.

Special Keys

Look at your keyboard and find the following keys:

 The Enter (or Return) key is one of the most frequently used keys on the keyboard. It is used to tell the computer to execute certain commands. It is also used in word processors to end paragraphs and insert blank lines within text.

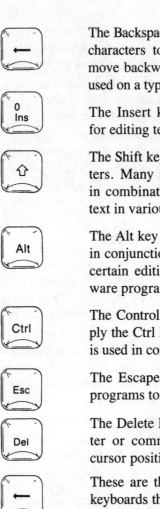

The Backspace key is used to delete unwanted characters to the left of the cursor, *not* to move backward through text, as it would be used on a typewriter.

The Insert key is used in word processors for editing text.

The Shift key is used to create uppercase letters. Many software programs use this key in combination with a function key to edit text in various ways.

The Alt key (Alt stands for alternate) is used in conjunction with function keys to execute certain editing or control functions in software programs.

The Control key (usually referred to as simply the Ctrl key), like the Alt and Shift keys, is used in conjunction with the function keys.

The Escape (or Esc) key is used by many programs to cancel a command input.

The Delete key erases or deletes the character or command that exists at the current cursor position.

These are the cursor arrow keys. On most keyboards these arrows are on the same keys as the numeric keypad numbers 2, 4, 6, and 8. The *cursor* is the small flashing underline character that indicates where the next character you type will appear. These keys allow you to move the cursor throughout a document without disturbing the text. The cursor cannot be moved with these arrow keys beyond the end of a document where no text or graphic input has been made.

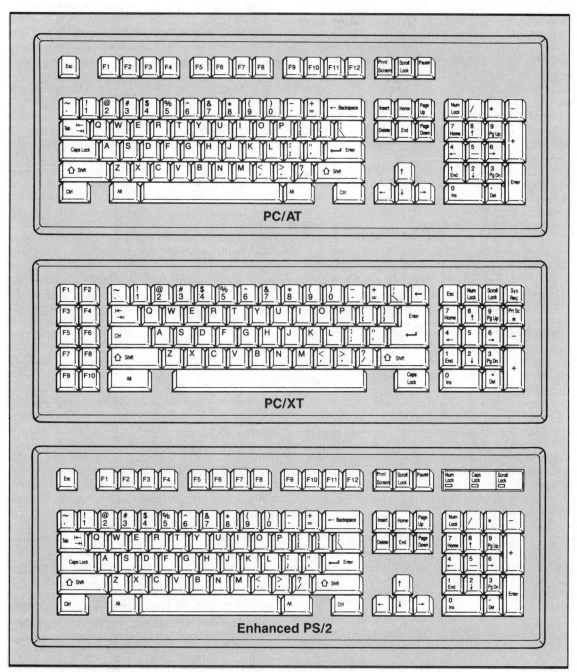

Figure 1.4: *The PC/AT, PC/XT, and enhanced PS/2 keyboard*

The Function Keys

The function keys are those keys labeled F1 through F10 or F12, depending on which style of keyboard you are using. They are along the top of the keyboard on newer styles or in two rows down the left side of the keyboard on the older styles. No matter what their location, they perform the same tasks.

These keys are programmed to perform the many complex tasks that are required in the software programs you use. Certain tasks are performed by pressing a function key by itself, others by pressing a function key in conjunction with the Shift, Alt, or Ctrl key.

The Printer

A computer, powerful as it may be, is limited without a printer. You can create beautiful documents, but if you can't transform them into hard copies, they are of no use to anyone beyond the reach of your computer. The three basic types of printers are dot-matrix, daisy-wheel, and laser printers. The second and third types are called letter-quality printers.

Dot-matrix printers print by grouping hundreds of small dots into the shape of the letters, numbers, characters, or graphics that make up the document. The print clarity depends on the number of dots per square inch. The edges of the printed characters, if you look closely, will appear ragged. Consequently, documents printed on these printers are mainly rough drafts, lists, memos, and graphics. Though there are dot-matrix printers that approach letter-quality text, most formal documents should be printed on a letter-quality printer.

There are two types of letter-quality printers—the daisy-wheel printer and the laser printer. A daisy-wheel printer prints the same way an electric typewriter does. A circular plastic print element (the daisy wheel) strikes an inked ribbon to place the characters on the page. These printers are generally slow, noisy, and limited to printing text only. Graphics cannot be printed with a daisy-wheel printer.

The laser printer provides high-quality lettering and clean, sharp graphics. They are also fast and relatively quiet, helping to increase efficiency and reduce noise fatigue. The laser printer is used for desktop publishing because it can accommodate many different font styles and sophisticated graphics programs.

Chances are you won't have a printer hooked up to your computer if you are working on the Novell network. Usually the printers are hooked up to the central computer that runs the network, probably in the data processing center. If you aren't sure which types of printers are installed on your Novell system, ask your supervisor what type they are and to show you their location.

The Mouse

A mouse is a small, hand-held object connected to your computer by a thin cord. If you have a mouse connected to your system, it will be sitting next to your computer. Mice are usually either rectangular or oval and may have two or three buttons. Look at Figure 1.5. If you use your imagination, the body of the device resembles the body of a mouse, and the cord looks like its tail.

The mouse is used to move a small arrow or other such indicator that appears on your monitor screen and, in effect, does the same job as the cursor keys, only much faster. The indicator is moved across the screen by sliding the mouse over a flat surface (some mice use a special, light-sensitive pad); the screen indicator moves in the same direction as the mouse. You can select and activate program features by using the mouse to place the screen pointer on a menu item or icon

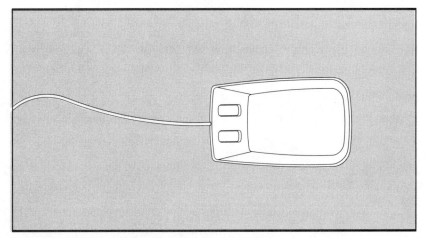

Figure 1.5: *A typical mouse*

(a graphic representation of a program feature) and pressing the correct mouse button. You also can use the mouse to create and edit graphics in a graphics program.

Software Programs

As powerful as the physical components that make up a computer system may be, they will not process any information until you install the necessary software programs. These programs are written in sophisticated computer languages and electronically recorded onto floppy disks for sale and distribution.

Software programs exist for practically any job you may encounter. The most common categories are word processing, database management, spreadsheets, and desktop publishing. Other categories include accounting and payroll, finance, networking programs (like Novell NetWare), telecommunications, graphics, and even computer games.

The next few sections give a brief overview of some software programs that you will encounter most often.

The Disk Operating System

The *disk operating system,* referred to as DOS, electronically configures the CPU's microchips so they can correctly interpret and execute the programs you wish to run on your computer. DOS is also a management tool, providing a file maintenance system and coordinating the complex movement of information between all the components of your computer system. Without this program your computer will do nothing except take up space on your desk.

If you have a hard disk in your CPU, DOS will already be installed. When you turn your computer on, DOS is automatically loaded into the computer. This process is known as *booting* the system. Once this is done, you can load your programs and begin work. Floppy-disk users must insert a floppy disk with the DOS program on it into their floppy-disk drive in order to boot the system and begin work. Refer to Chapter 3 for a more detailed explanation of DOS functions.

*A*pplication Programs

Even if you are new to computers, you've undoubtedly heard about the remarkable capabilities of these sophisticated machines. These capabilities are packaged into what are known as *application programs*. Most of these programs have been developed for the many needs of the business world. The remainder of this chapter briefly describes what these programs can do for you.

There are five basic types of applications you should be familiar with: word processing, spreadsheets, database management, accounting and payroll, and desktop publishing.

Word Processors

A word processor is a program containing powerful features that allow you to create, edit, and organize your documents more efficiently and effectively than you could on a typewriter. Setting margins and tabs, selecting line spacing, centering text, hyphenating words, and numbering pages are just a few of the formatting decisions that must be made when preparing any document. With a word processing application, all these features, and many more, are available with a few keystrokes. WordPerfect, the most popular word processing program, lists approximately 500 features on its Help menu. See Chapter 9, "Learning the Basics of WordPerfect," for an introduction to WordPerfect 5.

Editing, often difficult on a typewriter, is a much simpler task on a word processor, which allows you to edit an entire document before you print a single page. You can delete any amount of unwanted text, from a single letter up to many pages, and replace it with new text. With a few keystrokes you can select any amount of text and copy it or move it to another location in the same, or another, document. You can print one page, selected pages, or the entire document. Also, in most cases, what you see on your screen is what your document will look like when it is printed. These are just a few of the many features word processors offer.

Spreadsheets

Spreadsheet applications are an invaluable aid when your work requires preparing budgets, accounts payable and receivable reports, stock analysis reports, income statements, production schedules, and other similar tasks. Any project that requires numerical listings can be accomplished on a spreadsheet. Once these listings are completed, the program allows you to perform mathematical functions on the numbers, including addition, subtraction, multiplication, division, trigonometrical and statistical functions, and business calculations.

The features available in most spreadsheet applications are too numerous to mention here, but one of the most exciting allows you to ask the question, "What if?" What will be the effect on the company's net profit if I raise salaries? What if I increase the price of this item and place another item on sale? Once you have created a spreadsheet to show the current financial status of some part or parts of a business, you can change numerical values, using a hypothetical situation, and the program will recalculate and adjust your previous values based on the new input. This feature is very beneficial when you are developing strategies for future business ventures.

Lotus 1-2-3 is one of the largest selling spreadsheet programs, and I have included some beginner exercises in Chapter 10, "Learning the Basics of Lotus 1-2-3."

Database Management

A database is a body of information systematically organized for quick reference. Databases can be as small as a personal telephone directory or as large as a listing of all the books in the Library of Congress. With a database management program you can create and edit a database, search for and display the information in that database in a variety of ways, perform mathematical calculations on numerical databases, and print the results. The types of databases that can be created are limited only by your imagination and your needs.

dBASE IV is a popular database manager used by many businesses. Chapter 11, "Learning the Basics of dBASE IV," guides you through some beginning exercises in the construction of a database.

Accounting and Payroll

Many businesses, especially small ones, cannot afford to have a separate accounting department, and hiring an outside firm to handle the accounting and payroll requirements is also expensive. Usually the boss or a secretary with some accounting experience is assigned the job of bookkeeping. These people often have other duties to perform, and minding the books can be very time consuming. An accounting and payroll application is just the answer for streamlining this area of the business.

A good accounting application can handle tasks such as accounts receivable and payable, sales orders, state and federal taxes, time and billing, and purchase orders. Many of these programs are designed to work with spreadsheet and database programs such as Lotus 1-2-3 and dBASE IV.

Desktop Publishing

Desktop publishing programs put you in the same league as professional typesetters and printers. If you need to produce newsletters, create forms, place graphics into a document, create multicolumn documents, or work on any project that requires integrating word processing, graphics, typesetting, and page layout, then these programs are the answer. Another benefit is that no experience in typesetting is required to produce professional-looking documents.

Some advanced word processing programs, such as WordPerfect, incorporate many desktop publishing features. They allow you to import graphics from many sources, do layouts in various measurement units, choose from a large selection of type styles, and display the results on the screen exactly as the document will appear on the printed page.

If your job requires layout and design work, you may be using one of the two most popular desktop publishing applications, Ventura Publisher and PageMaker.

*B*acking Up Your Software

If your computer has a hard disk, you will want to copy the application onto the hard disk before using it. If you have a computer that has a floppy-disk drive and no hard disk, you should make a backup copy of the application. Once you've done this, put the original disk in a safe place and use the backup copy as your working copy. Floppy disks are sensitive and damage easily, and hard disks have been known to fail, or "crash." Having backup copies of your programs can be a lifesaver. See Chapter 3 for instructions on how to make a backup copy of a floppy disk using the DISKCOPY and COPY commands.

Summary

In this chapter you were introduced to the hardware components that make up a personal computer system. The CPU is the power-house of the system, running programs and communicating with such peripheral components as the monitor, keyboard, printer, and mouse. You learned about hard- and floppy-disk drives and how these drives operate the disks that store your valuable data. You also learned about the special keys on the computer keyboard and their use.

You learned about the kinds of software programs that can run on your computer system. The disk operating system, DOS, must be loaded into the computer before any software applications can be run. Once DOS is installed, you can create documents on a word proces-sor, crunch numbers in a spreadsheet program, build a comprehensive database with a database manager, create your own newsletters with a desktop publishing application, and keep track of finances with a pay-roll and accounting program.

In Chapter 2 you will learn about computer memory, an often mis-understood subject (especially by beginners), but important and really quite simple.

NOVELL NETWARE

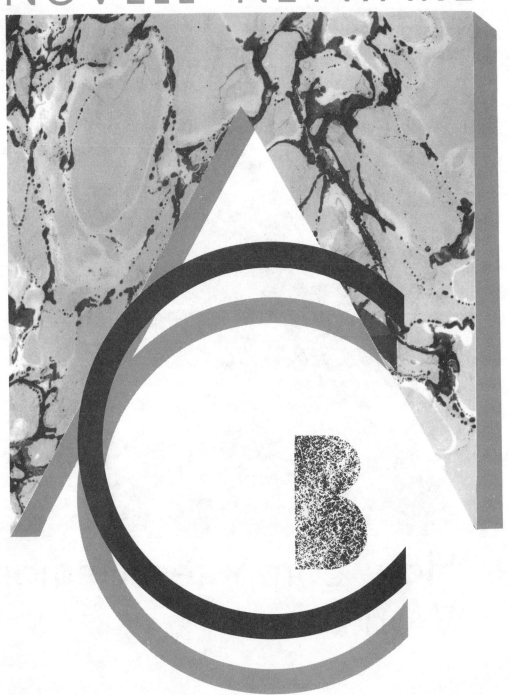

2

How Computer Memory
Works

A basic understanding of how computer memory works is important if you are to operate effectively in a computer environment. Don't worry, I'm not going to confuse you with technical language. But there are a few things you should be aware of that will help you better understand what is going on inside that machine sitting on your desk.

Every computer has some method of remembering commands and data entered into the system. When you run an application program such as a word processor, the program's operational codes are loaded into the computer's memory. Once this happens, the computer can take the data typed into the system and manipulate it according to the program's abilities.

Here's an example of what happens when you enter data from the keyboard. When you create words by pressing the letter keys, coded signals are sent to the computer's memory, where they are electronically interpreted and displayed as corresponding letters on the monitor screen: you type the letter *z*, and you instantly see the letter *z* on your screen. The screen presents a display of the data held in the computer memory. The computer will remember this input until you delete it from the memory or turn the computer off.

There are several kinds of memory operating in your computer, some of which are beyond the scope of this book. In this chapter you will learn about the basic types of computer memory that are important to you and your work.

*R*andom Access Memory

Random access memory, called RAM for short, is the area of the computer where your initial input of data is stored. RAM is referred to as *temporary memory*. You've already learned that every CPU contains many integrated circuits commonly called microchips. These tiny chips, about one-fourth of a square inch in size, are the brain of the computer. Because of them, your desktop computer packs more power than older computers that filled an entire room.

When you turn your computer on, electricity energizes the microchips. Then, information is loaded into these energized microchips when the computer runs a software application, reads information off a data disk, or receives input from the keyboard. The data is electronically stored within the chips where it awaits future processing commands. Without the electrical charge, the chips are inert and empty. If the flow of electricity is interrupted for any reason, the data held in the microchips disappears along with the electrical charge. This is why RAM is known as temporary memory.

A simple way to think of RAM is to visualize your electronic data moving around in an organized manner inside your monitor. You can see portions of this data displayed on your screen. If your computer shuts down for any reason, that data disappears from the monitor screen (and from RAM) and is lost forever.

To protect this data, you can save it into what's known as *permanent storage*, which will be discussed shortly.

*H*ow Much Memory Exists in RAM?

This question is important because every software application requires a certain amount of RAM in order to operate effectively. The amount will normally not concern you since your computer system will probably have been set up by your supervisor. But you should be aware of this concept in case you ever get a message on your screen indicating that there isn't enough memory to execute a program. If this happens, you will have to unload a program that may be taking up space in RAM.

How much RAM you have depends on the model of computer and its configuration. Here is a list of some common IBM models and how much RAM they contain. The amounts are given in kilobytes (K), with one kilobyte being equal to approximately 1,000 bytes. One byte equals one character of text.

Model	Memory
IBM PC	64K or 256K
IBM PC-XT	256K
IBM PC-XT clone/compatible	640K
IBM PC-AT	256K or 512K
IBM PC-AT clone/compatible	512K or 640K

Can you increase your RAM? The answer is yes. You can purchase add-on boards that are inserted into expansion slots inside your CPU. In a moment, you'll know more about expanding your computer's memory.

Why have temporary memory if you can easily lose all your hard work with one power interruption? Wouldn't it be safer to record data permanently, at the same time you create it? The subject of permanent storage is covered in the next section, but the reason for temporary memory has to do with speed of processing. The information in RAM exists as electronically-coded signals, and therefore it can be processed and manipulated as fast as electricity moves through the circuits, which is at approximately half the speed of light. This allows rapid accomplishment of complex tasks, which is the primary reason for using a computer.

Remember, data stored in temporary memory exists in a volatile state, so it's vital that you protect your data against inadvertent or accidental loss. You need a method of permanent storage.

What Is Permanent Storage?

Permanent storage is accomplished by physically recording information stored in RAM onto a floppy or hard disk. This recording process is called *saving* and is essential when creating documents with the computer. (Refer to Chapter 3 for more details on saving.) Saving a document is similar to recording your favorite song while it is playing on the radio. If you do nothing more than listen to the song, it will be gone when it has finished playing, but if you record it on tape, you can listen to it as often as you want. Remember, if you turn your computer off, or if it loses power before you save your document, you will lose everything that was not saved.

What happens when you save a document that is temporarily stored in RAM? The data is physically recorded by implanting electronically-coded signals onto a hard or floppy disk. When you are ready to retrieve the saved document, the computer is directed to read the recorded signals, make a copy of the data, and load it back into RAM. Making a copy of the data is an important point. Although your document appears on your monitor screen, indicating it has returned to RAM, a copy of it remains stored on the disk. If you lose power to the computer, and therefore lose the retrieved document located in RAM, you still have the original copy available on the disk.

I recommend you save your work in 10-minute intervals. It's less damaging to lose 10 minutes' worth of effort than an hour's worth. Many application programs will automatically save your work for you at a time interval of your choosing. If power to your PC is interrupted while you are in the middle of editing a document, you can recover everything up to the last automatic save. This feature has saved me on more than one occasion.

Memory-Resident Programs

The term *memory-resident* (or *terminate and stay resident*, TSR) applies to programs that are stored in RAM at the same time another application is running. Some memory-resident programs remain hidden until you activate them. For instance, suppose you're a secretary and you use a word processor every day. You also use a memory-resident dictionary that is stored in RAM. Without exiting the word processor, you can press designated keys that activate the dictionary, which then appears on your screen. You look up the needed definition, exit from the dictionary, and return directly to your document. The dictionary program remains in RAM until you activate it again. Other memory-resident programs, once loaded, do not require keystrokes to activate them; they may be doing tasks "in the background" while you work with another application.

Because memory-resident programs use up a portion of your temporary memory, you can easily run out of memory if you load too many memory-resident programs at the same time. This is a good reason to have as much RAM as possible.

Adding Memory to Your Computer

DOS imposes a 640K limit on RAM. There are, however, ways to get around this limitation. In addition to the add-on boards that increase normal RAM up to a maximum of 640K, there are boards that allow you to add from 512K to 16 megabytes (M) of memory (1 megabyte equals 1,048,576 bytes). This additional memory can be used only by programs that are specifically written to do so. Programs that take advantage of expanded memory are Lotus 1-2-3, Symphony, Paradox, AutoCAD, and R:base System V, to name just a few. As a network user you probably will not be concerned with additional memory, but knowing it exists could be useful if you find you need more RAM.

Summary

In this chapter you learned about temporary memory (RAM) and permanent memory. Remember, data in temporary memory is lost if there is an interruption of power to the computer. Save your data frequently by writing it into permanent memory on a hard or floppy disk. If you overload your RAM, look to see if there are any memory-resident programs operating behind the scenes that you can unload. You may never need expanded or extended memory, but it's good to know it's available if your work calls for a greater amount of RAM.

The next chapter introduces you to the different ways you can put DOS to work organizing the information you store in the computer. This is an important chapter, one that I think you'll find interesting.

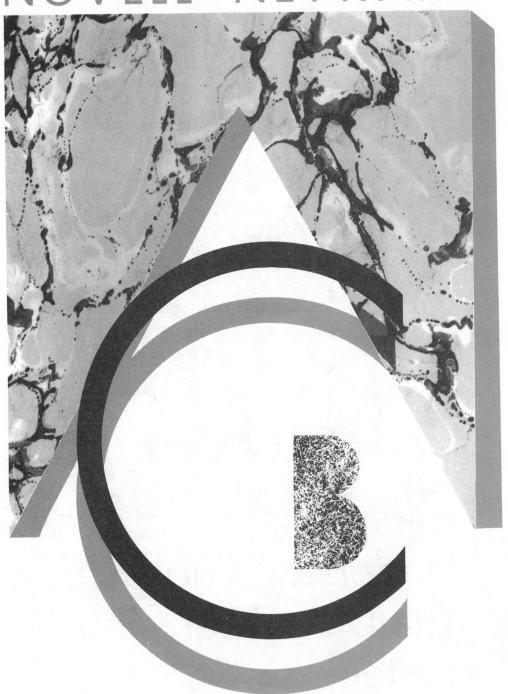

Understanding DOS: The Disk Operating System

The disk operating system, DOS, has two components. The first component you learned about in Chapter 1: the system that electronically configures the microchips in the CPU so that you can run your software applications. The second component of DOS is commonly referred to as *DOS commands*. DOS commands are the tools with which you manage your computer's functions and create the organizational structure that is necessary for the orderly storing of document files and application programs.

The NetWare network operating system works hand in hand with DOS, and therefore, in order to work effectively on the network, it is important that you have a basic understanding of how DOS operates. This chapter describes some important rules and procedures for operating DOS effectively.

Some DOS Rules

You must know some basic DOS principles before you begin using DOS commands, especially if you are a beginner.

- You can use either uppercase or lowercase letters when typing a DOS command.

- After typing a DOS command, you must press the Enter key in order to execute the command.

- Use the Backspace key to correct typing errors.

- An incorrectly typed command will result in the screen message

  Bad command or file name

  and return you to the DOS prompt.

- DOS memorizes the last typed command. Pressing the F3 key automatically retypes this command at the DOS prompt. This feature saves time when you have to repeat DOS commands.

- Use DOS commands carefully to avoid accidents such as deleting important files or reformatting your hard disk, thereby losing all your files.

*S*tarting Your Computer

There are basically three ways to configure the disk drives installed in a computer system that is connected to a network, and each configuration has a slightly different start-up procedure. The hands-on exercises in this chapter will be easier to do if you can operate your computer as an independent workstation separate from the Novell networking environment. This is a simple matter if you follow the start-up procedures outlined in this section.

However, if you have a *diskless workstation* (one that has neither a hard disk nor a floppy disk), you cannot operate your computer as an independent workstation. This is because when you start a diskless workstation, you are automatically entered into the network and must use the network operating system, not DOS. In order to do the exercises in this chapter, those of you with diskless workstations will need to borrow someone else's computer that has a disk drive. If you're unable to do so, be sure to read through this chapter anyway; the information presented here will be helpful when you work through the exercises in Chapter 4.

*T*he DOS Prompt

Before going through the start-up procedures for your computer, you need to understand some things about the DOS prompt. All communication with DOS is done at a *DOS prompt*, where all DOS commands are entered.

A DOS prompt displays the name of the disk drive that the computer is logged on to. Floppy-disk drives are labeled A and B when you have two drives. If there is only one floppy-disk drive, it's called drive A. When you log on to drive A, your screen will display a DOS prompt that looks like this:

    A>

When you log on to drive B, the prompt will look like this:

    B>

A hard disk may be divided into one or more drives, depending on its size. The primary drive is called drive C. Secondary drives are called drives D and E. Screen prompts for these drives look like this:

C>

D>

E>

It is possible for a workstation to have up to five local drives: two floppy drives, A and B, and a hard disk configured into three drives, C, D, and E. This is not the norm, however, so don't feel cheated if you only have one or two. Many networking systems have diskless workstations that don't have even one local disk drive.

The Novell network has its own system for assigning drive letters. These network drives are not physical drives, like the local work-station drives, but are used to identify the network directories where data is stored on a large hard disk installed on a central computer called a *file server*. (You will learn more about the file server, net-work drives, network directories, and other network components in Part II.) Networks that use DOS version 3.0 and above have network drive designations that start with F and proceed all the way to Z. For DOS versions 2.0 through 3.0, the network drives begin with D. On a diskless workstation, the first network drive is drive A.

Usually a workstation will automatically enter the network when you turn it on. Floppy-disk users will have special instructions on their start-up DOS disk and hard-disk users will have these instructions on their hard disk. However, for the following exercises, I would like you to *not* be in the network. Both hard-disk and floppy-disk users should ask the network supervisor for a DOS disk without any instructions for entering the network before beginning these exercises.

*S*tarting the Computer *from a Hard- or Floppy-Disk Drive*

1. Place the floppy disk with the DOS program files on it in drive A.

2. Turn the computer on. DOS is loaded into RAM.

3. If you see a date and time prompt, type in the correct date and time, pressing the Enter key after each entry. When you see

the A> on the screen, you're ready to work with programs and data stored on disks placed in drive A.

Don't turn your computer off—in a moment you'll enter a command at the DOS prompt.

*C*hanging to Another Disk Drive

Hard-disk users can change between drive A and drive C on the hard disk (also drives D and E if the hard disk is partitioned into these extra drive designations). If you have a second floppy disk on your computer, you can also change to drive B. Dual floppy-disk users can only change between drive A and B.

To change from one drive to another, type the desired drive letter followed by a colon and press the Enter key. On a hard-disk computer, you are currently logged onto drive A, and the screen displays the DOS prompt A>. Let's change to drive C and back to drive A.

1. Be sure a floppy disk with the DOS program files is in drive A. If you have a low-density disk drive you cannot use a high-density disk. A low-density disk, however, will work in a high-density drive.

2. Type **C:** and press the Enter key.

The DOS prompt changes to C>, and you are now logged onto drive C where you can access information from any directory on this drive. Now change back to drive A.

3. Type **A:** and press the Enter key.

On a dual floppy-disk computer you should have an A> displayed on your screen after starting up. The DOS disk must stay in drive A. Let's change to drive B and return to drive A.

1. Place any floppy disk that has some data recorded on it in drive B.

2. Type **B:** and press the Enter key.

The DOS prompt changes to B>. You are now logged onto the B drive. Now change back to drive A.

3. Type **A:** and press the Enter key.

If you forget to place a floppy disk into an A or B drive and attempt to log on to that drive, you might receive this message:

Not ready error reading drive A (B)
Abort, Retry, Fail?

Simply place a floppy disk that has some information written on it into the A or B drive and press the R key to retry.

Please keep your computer on while you read these next few pages.

Getting Organized

Organizing the data that is stored in your computer is absolutely necessary. Because it is possible to store thousands of documents on a hard disk, you must be able to locate the documents you need quickly, when you need them. DOS provides an efficient system of organization, and a working understanding of this system is vital.

This section will familiarize you with the organizational techniques available with your computer. You'll learn about root directories, directories, and subdirectories and how to assign file names to your documents prior to saving them into these directories. You will also learn the importance of thinking in terms of location when you need to tell the computer to locate and retrieve a stored document in one of the many directories that may exist on a storage disk.

The Computer as a File Cabinet

In order to direct the computer to find the documents you have stored, certain commands must be entered. You must tell the computer exactly where to look and what to look for. If you aren't exact in your description, the computer will not give you the document you want.

You know how a conventional file cabinet works: the cabinet holds file drawers in which there may be file folders in which are stored files. When maintained properly, a file cabinet is an organizational tool of great value.

Your computer can be thought of as an electronic filing system. You can organize and store literally thousands of files on either floppy or hard disks, which can be thought of as electronic file cabinets. When you need a particular document, you simply direct the computer to look first in the correct file cabinet, then in the correct file drawer, followed by the correct file folder, find the correct file, and retrieve it. This is a space-saving method of storing large numbers of files very efficiently. But don't throw away your regular filing cabinets; you still need a place to store hard copies of your documents.

*D*irectories: DOS's Filing System

An ordinary filing cabinet usually has file drawers labeled according to a particular subject area and contains all the files dealing with that subject area. Well, file drawers can be created within the computer, too. These drawers are called *directories*.

DOS automatically creates a main directory that includes all the available storage space on a hard or floppy disk. This directory is called the *root directory* and is like an electronic filing cabinet. A root directory is represented by the backslash (\). If you study your keyboard for a moment, you'll find a key with the \ symbol on it. The root directory for a hard disk will most often be represented as *C:*, the root directory for the C drive. Depending on the kind of computer system you have, you may see a *D:* or an *E:* when a hard disk is electronically partitioned into smaller areas and assigned these drive letters. On a floppy disk, the root directory is represented by an *A:* or *B:*, depending on which drive the disk is in. The letter and the colon represent the disk drive and the \ character represents the root directory.

To further refine the organization of your electronic filing cabinet, you can divide the root directory into smaller directories. These directories, corresponding to file drawers in a conventional filing cabinet, are created to store files that pertain to a specific subject area. If you wish to break down the file organization into even smaller subject areas, it's possible to create *subdirectories* within these directories, which would correspond to file folders in a file drawer. It is also a good idea to assign directory names that describe the kinds of files stored within them. See Figure 3.1 for an illustration of a DOS filing system.

Hard disks get organized into directories more often than floppy disks because of their immense storage capacity. You can create directories on floppy disks, but, because their storage space is limited, this is seldom done.

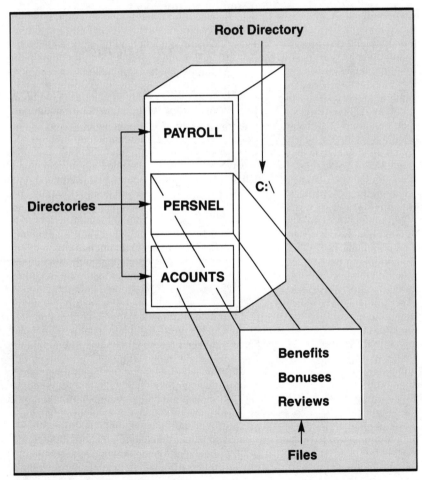

Figure 3.1: *An electronic file cabinet*

*N*aming Files

The lowest level of organization is the file. DOS will not allow you to save a document unless you assign a specific file name to it. Without a unique file name, it would be next to impossible to locate a document once it was saved into permanent storage. It is helpful to assign a file name that readily identifies the subject matter of the document. A file name may also include an extension to the primary name to further help identify the file.

Table 3.1 lists four rules, with examples, that must be followed when assigning a name to a file.

Using File Name Extensions

Use *extensions* to aid in identifying a file's contents. The effective use of file name extensions is an excellent organizational tool. Creating separate and unique names for each file may become difficult as the number of files increases. Creative use of extensions allows you to use the same primary file name several times, tagged with its own unique extension. Common extensions can be created to categorize files into subject areas. For instance, you could use the extension .LTR for letters, .DOC for documents, .RPT for reports, .LST for lists, and so on. Your file names may be limited to eight characters

Table 3.1: *File-Naming Conventions*

Rule	Example
A file name may be from one to eight characters in length and may begin with a letter or a number.	1BIZLTR PERSFILE
Lowercase letters may be used when typing file names.	rules.doc census.dat
A file name may not contain a space.	PALMTREE HILITER
Never use the following symbols in a file name: < > : ; = [ ] * , " + ?¦ \ /	

with a three-character extension, but only your imagination limits how you use them.

It is important to be familiar with several common extensions that software programmers use when naming files used in software applications. Never change these extensions, or you may disable your program and render it useless. Also, never use these extensions in naming your own files. Table 3.2 lists the extensions to avoid using. Refer to your DOS reference manual for a more complete list of commonly used file name extensions. Several common extensions for graphics files are also listed for those of you who will be working with graphics programs. It is important to always use these extensions to identify the type of graphic file you are using in a document and never change them.

Table 3.2: *Reserved File Name Extensions*

Extension	Description
.EXE	An executable file. These files contain the instructions that tell the computer to run a software program.
.COM	An executable file for simple programs such as DOS commands.
.BAT	Batch files. These files contain instructions for DOS to automatically accomplish certain functions.
.BAK	Backup file extension assigned when a file is automatically backed up.
.WK1	Spreadsheet file extension.
Graphics File Extensions	
.PIC	Lotus 1-2-3 PIC format
.PCXPC	Paintbrush format
.TIF	Tagged Image File format
.WPG	WordPerfect Graphics format
.IMG	GEM Paint format

Tips on File Organization

Well-organized files will make it easier to perform your work more efficiently. I suggest you write down all the tasks that you do on the computer. Break these tasks into different subject areas and develop a scheme for naming files that relates to each area. Subject areas could include letters, lists, inventories, payroll, accounts receivable, memos, and personnel. Remember these subject areas; they will be helpful in designing your filing system.

Using DOS Commands

In this section you'll learn about the basic DOS commands that will enable you to work with directories, format floppy disks, make copies of data disks, and copy and delete files. DOS is a very powerful system with many exotic commands, many of which are beyond the scope of this book. However, every level of user should be aware of eight of the most frequently used commands. These eight commands, listed and described in Table 3.3, are the basic tools needed to effectively organize your data and move about the computer.

Table 3.3: Eight Frequently Used DOS Commands

Command	Description
DIR, DIR/P, and DIR/W	Displays a list of files in a directory
MD	Creates new directories
CD	Moves from one directory to another
RD	Deletes directories
DEL	Deletes files
FORMAT	Prepares new disks so they will accept data
DISKCOPY	Makes backup copies of disks
COPY	Copies files from one location to another

Your computer should be turned on and DOS loaded into RAM. You should see your base prompt (A>, C>, or F>) on the monitor screen. If not, go to "Starting Your Computer" earlier in this chapter and follow the instructions for your computer.

In the following exercises the drive prompt will not be shown when a DOS command is being described.

Displaying Files in a Directory (DIR, DIR/P, DIR/W)

The Directory List command (DIR) displays a list of all the files stored in a particular directory. The names of subdirectories attached to that directory are also included in the list. Let's use the DIR command to generate a file list. If you shut your computer down after finishing the previous exercises, please restart using the floppy disk that contains the DOS program files without the network entry instructions. The following exercise is for both hard-disk and dual floppy-disk users.

1. Place the DOS Program disk in drive A and turn on your computer.

2. If necessary, respond to the date and time prompts.

3. At the A>, type **DIR** and press the Enter key.

The complete list of all the DOS files scroll onto the screen. See Figure 3.2 for a sample list of DOS files (your list may differ).

Notice the file list includes information about the file size (in bytes), date of creation or last edit, file extension, and the time it was saved. This information can be useful to help identify files.

If there are a great many files, as there are in this example, the complete list of files will not be visible on the screen all at once. Two DOS commands alleviate this problem—the DIR/P and DIR/W commands. Let's look at these two commands.

1. The DOS prompt should still be displayed on your screen. Type **DIR/P** and press the Enter key.

At the DOS prompt you see a *partial* list of the files displayed on the screen, as in Figure 3.3. You are shown one screen of files at a time, beginning with the first files in the list.

Notice the prompt at the bottom of the screen telling you to press any key when ready. When you do so, you'll see the next screen listing the next sequence of files.

2. Press any key as many times as necessary to list the remaining files until you return to the DOS prompt.

Now let's look at the DIR/W command.

```
ASSIGN   COM    1530   7-24-87  12:00a
ATTRIB   EXE   10656   7-24-87  12:00a
AUTOEXEC BAT     159   4-01-89  10:36a
CAPTURE  COM    5918   9-16-87   2:03a
CHKDSK   COM    9819   7-24-87  12:00a
COMP     COM    4183   7-24-87  12:00a
CONFIG   SYS      50  12-20-88   2:59p
COPY            1647   7-24-87  12:00a
COUNTRY  SYS   11254   7-24-87  12:00a
DEBUG    COM   15866   7-24-87  12:00a
DISKCOMP COM    5848   7-24-87  12:00a
DISKCOPY COM    6264   7-24-87  12:00a
DISPLAY  SYS   11259   7-24-87  12:00a
DRIVER   SYS    1165   7-24-87  12:00a
EDLIN    COM    7495   7-24-87  12:00a
EGA      CPI   49065   7-24-87  12:00a
EXE2BIN  EXE    3050   7-24-87  12:00a
FASTOPEN EXE    3888   7-24-87  12:00a
FC       EXE   15974   7-24-87  12:00a
FDISK    COM   48919   7-24-87  12:00a
FIND     EXE    6403   7-24-87  12:00a
FRECOVER DAT    5632   5-08-89   7:57p
       27 File(s)    19456 bytes free

A>
```

Figure 3.2: *File list displayed with the DIR command*

```
     .          <DIR>          2-10-88  12:32p
     ..         <DIR>          2-10-88  12:32p
COMMAND  COM   25276   7-24-87  12:00a
4201     CPI   17089   7-24-87  12:00a
5202     CPI     459   7-24-87  12:00a
ANSI     SYS    1647   7-24-87  12:00a
APPEND   EXE    5794   7-24-87  12:00a
ASSIGN   COM    1530   7-24-87  12:00a
ATTRIB   EXE   10656   7-24-87  12:00a
CHKDSK   COM    9819   7-24-87  12:00a
COMP     COM    4183   7-24-87  12:00a
COUNTRY  SYS   11254   7-24-87  12:00a
DISKCOMP COM    5848   7-24-87  12:00a
DISKCOPY COM    6264   7-24-87  12:00a
DISPLAY  SYS   11259   7-24-87  12:00a
DRIVER   SYS    1165   7-24-87  12:00a
EDLIN    COM    7495   7-24-87  12:00a
EXE2BIN  EXE    3050   7-24-87  12:00a
FASTOPEN EXE    3888   7-24-87  12:00a
FDISK    COM   48919   7-24-87  12:00a
FIND     EXE    6403   7-24-87  12:00a
FORMAT   COM   11671   7-24-87  12:00a
GRAFTABL COM    6136   7-24-87  12:00a
Strike a key when ready . . . _
```

Figure 3.3: *File list displayed with the DIR/P command*

3. At the DOS prompt, type **DIR/W** and press the Enter key.

Figure 3.4 shows a list of files spread horizontally across the screen. This display does not provide the size, date, and time information, but it does allow more files to be seen on the screen.

The DIR commands—DIR, DIR/P, and DIR/W—are helpful when you need to locate a file, check for the correct spelling of a file name, determine the size of the file, or verify the date and time a file was created or edited.

*C*reating Directories (MD)

The best way to learn about directories is to create them yourself. Remember, directories are the "file drawers" in your electronic file cabinet, the places where you will store your files when you create them. In this section you will use the Make Directory command (MD) to create two directories that you'll use in some of the exercises in this section.

The first task is to think of a name for the directory. (Follow the rules for naming files (Table 3.1); some keyboard characters are not usable when naming directories.) The example uses the name PAYROLL, but you can use any name you wish.

Hard-disk users should change to drive C by typing **C:** and pressing the Enter key. Floppy-disk users should still be located on drive A.

```
A>DIR/W

Volume in drive A has no label
Directory of  A:\

COMMAND  COM     APPEND   EXE     4201     CPI     5202     CPI     ANSI     SYS
ASSIGN   COM     ATTRIB   EXE     AUTOEXEC BAT     CAPTURE  COM     CHKDSK   COM
COMP     COM     CONFIG   SYS     COPY             COUNTRY  SYS     DEBUG    COM
DISKCOMP COM     DISKCOPY COM     DISPLAY  SYS     DRIVER   SYS     EDLIN    COM
EGA      CPI     EXE2BIN  EXE     FASTOPEN EXE     FC       EXE     FDISK    COM
FIND     EXE     FRECOVER DAT
       27 File(s)     19456 bytes free

A>
```

Figure 3.4: *File list displayed with the DIR/W command*

1. At the DOS prompt, type **CD** and press the Enter key. This ensures you are located at the root directory. (You will learn about the Change Directory command (CD) in detail in the next exercise.)

2. Type **MD PAYROLL** and press the Enter key.

3. Type **MD ACCOUNTS** and press the Enter key.

The screen returns to the DOS prompt as though nothing happened, but the PAYROLL and ACCOUNTS directories do exist. Use the DIR command to verify.

4. Type **DIR** and press the Enter key. You should see the two new directories listed at the end of the list of files and directories stored on the root directory.

Figure 3.5 shows you an example of the new directory listing, which now includes PAYROLL and ACCOUNTS. Note the <DIR> notation after the directory name, specifying that this is a directory, not a file.

Remember, you can create new subdirectories off of either the PAYROLL or the ACCOUNTS directory if you need to break these directories into smaller file storage areas. To do this, change to the desired directory and then use the MD command to name a new subdirectory.

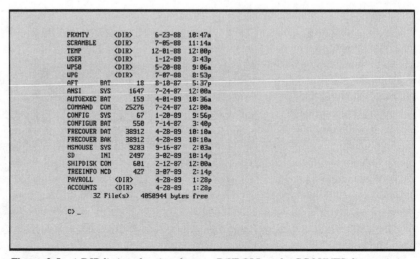

```
PRXMTY      <DIR>         6-23-88   10:47a
SCRAMBLE    <DIR>         7-05-88   11:14a
TEMP        <DIR>        12-01-88   12:00p
USER        <DIR>         1-12-89    3:43p
UP50        <DIR>         5-20-88    9:06a
UPG         <DIR>         7-07-88    8:53p
AFT    BAT        18      8-10-87    5:37p
ANSI   SYS      1647      7-24-87   12:00a
AUTOEXEC BAT     159      4-01-89   10:36a
COMMAND COM    25276      7-24-87   12:00a
CONFIG SYS        67      1-20-89    9:56p
CONFIGUR BAT     550      7-14-87    3:40p
FRECOVER DAT   38912      4-28-89   10:10a
FRECOVER BAK   38912      4-28-89   10:10a
MSMOUSE SYS     9283      9-16-87    2:03a
SD     INI      2497      3-02-89   10:14p
SHIPDISK COM     601      2-12-87   12:00a
TREEINFO NCD     427      3-07-89    2:14p
PAYROLL     <DIR>         4-28-89    1:28p
ACCOUNTS    <DIR>         4-28-89    1:28p
       32 File(s)   4050944 bytes free

C> _
```

Figure 3.5: *A DIR listing showing the new PAYROLL and ACCOUNTS directories*

*C*hanging Directories (CD)

The Change Directory command (CD) allows you to change from one directory to another. In order to be able to access the files stored in a particular directory, you must tell DOS to transfer you there. You will be changing directories often if you have a hard disk and when you work on the network, so this is an important command.

For this exercise, you should still be at the root directory. Let's change to the newly created PAYROLL directory.

1. At the DOS prompt type **CD PAYROLL** and press the Enter key.

2. Type **DIR** and press the Enter key. You are in the PAYROLL directory (see Figure 3.6).

When changing from the current directory to another directory that is not directly attached to the current directory, for example, from PAYROLL to ACCOUNTS, you must return to the root directory first and then change to the ACCOUNTS directory. Try it.

1. Type **CD** and press the Enter key. You return to the root directory. The backslash (\), when used by itself, stands for the root directory.

```
C>CD PAYROLL

C>DIR

    Volume in drive C is WOODWARD
    Directory of  C:\PAYROLL

    .           <DIR>     4-28-89   1:28p
    ..          <DIR>     4-28-89   1:28p
         2 File(s)   4028224 bytes free

C>_
```

Figure 3.6: *The PAYROLL directory*

2. Type **CD ACCOUNTS** and press the Enter key.

3. Type **DIR** and press the Enter key. The directory list shows you to be in the ACCOUNTS directory.

Whenever you're not sure which directory you're in, type **DIR** and look at the file list; the file names will usually clear up the dilemma.

A speedier way to move from one directory to another is to tell DOS to go to the root directory and automatically change to the desired directory. Let's see how this works. You are presently in the ACCOUNTS directory and want to move directly to the PAYROLL directory.

1. Type **CD\PAYROLL** and press the Enter key. You are immediately changed to the PAYROLL directory.

2. If you're not sure, type **DIR** and press the Enter key to verify you made the change.

Typing the backslash between CD and PAYROLL tells DOS to change to the root directory and then immediately change to the PAYROLL directory.

*R*emoving Directories (RD)

The Remove Directory command (RD) is used to delete a directory when it is no longer needed. Like the MD command, it is easy to use. Before you can remove a directory you must delete or move all the files and subdirectories contained in that directory. If you try to delete a directory before doing this, DOS will alert you with the prompt

**Invalid path, not directory,
or directory not empty**

This safeguards against inadvertently deleting valuable files stored in the directory.

Let's remove the ACCOUNTS directory from the root directory.

1. Type **CD** and press the Enter key. You are returned to the root directory.

2. Type **RD ACCOUNTS** and press the Enter key. The ACCOUNTS directory is no longer attached to the root directory.

3. Type **DIR** and press Enter to see a file list of the root directory. The PAYROLL directory is listed, the ACCOUNTS directory is gone.

Leave your computer on; you'll use it again in a few minutes to format some floppy disks.

*D*eleting Files from a Directory (DEL)

The Delete command is powerful and must be used cautiously so you don't inadvertently delete that important report you worked on for three weeks. However, you will want to purge old files that take up valuable storage space on a disk.

Before deleting a file, you need to change to the directory containing the file. Because your files are unique to the work you are doing, I'll show you the basic format for this command using a generalized file name called *FILENAME*. To delete an actual file, substitute your file's name where you see *FILENAME*.

At the DOS prompt, type **DEL *FILENAME*** and press the Enter key. That file will be deleted. You can use the asterisk wildcard symbol (*) to delete more than one file at a time. Let's say you want to delete three files with the same eight-letter name but different extensions, for example, *FILENAME.DOC*, *FILENAME.BAK*, and *FILENAME.TXT*. If you type **DEL FILENAME.*** and then press the Enter key, all the FILENAME files will be deleted, regardless of the extension name.

You can also use this procedure to delete a group of files with the same extension, for example, *LETTER.DOC*, *REPORT.DOC*, and *README.DOC*. If you type **DEL *.DOC** and press the Enter key, all the files with a .DOC extension will be deleted.

To use the wildcard symbol to delete every file in a directory, type **DEL *.*** and press the Enter key. You will be asked to verify the deletion with this prompt:

Are you sure (Y/N)?

Press **Y** and then the Enter key if you're sure you want to delete all the files in that directory. Press **N** followed by the Enter key if you want to check for important files before committing yourself to the deletion.

Be very careful when using the DEL command. Always mentally double-check before you press the Enter key to delete files. If you accidentally delete an important file, there are utility programs, such as Norton Utilities, that will recover the file. If you don't have access to such a utility, however, you will be out of luck.

Formatting Floppy Disks (FORMAT)

If you try to use a new floppy disk straight out of the box, you'll find your computer can't read it or write information onto it. It has to be formatted using the Disk Formatting command (FORMAT) first.

Formatting a floppy disk means placing recording tracks on it, similar to the grooves on a phonograph record. These grooves are electronic tracks that accept information generated within your computer's operating system. When this formatting is done, you can read and write data to that disk. If you want to use this disk in a computer using a different operating system, however, such as an Apple, it will not work, and you will have to reformat it for use on that system. If you reformat a disk for use in another system, you will erase any information recorded on the disk.

Formatting from a Hard-Disk Drive

Your computer should still be on from the previous exercises, and you should be located on drive C. Change to the directory (see "Changing Directories (CD)") that contains your DOS system files. This will normally be either the root directory on drive C or a DOS subdirectory. If you are not sure you have the right directory, use the DIR command to view the list of directory files and find the FORMAT.COM file. If you see this file listed, you are in the right directory.

1. Place a new floppy disk in drive A and close the latch.

2. At the C>, type **FORMAT A:** and press the Enter key. *Be sure* to type the A: or DOS will think you want to format the hard disk and will wipe out everything on drive C.

3. You will then be prompted with the following message:

   Insert new diskette for drive A:
   and strike ENTER when ready

   Press any key to format the disk. When the formatting operation is completed, you will see the screen shown in Figure 3.7.

4. If you want to format another disk, exchange the newly formatted disk in drive A with a new one and press **Y** followed by Enter. If you're done formatting, press **N** followed by the Enter key to return to the DOS prompt.

Formatting from a Floppy-Disk Drive

Your computer should be on from the last exercise. If it's not, place your DOS disk (without any network instructions) in drive A, close the latch, and turn the computer on and boot the system.

1. If you have two floppy-disk drives, place a new disk in drive B.

2. At the DOS prompt, type **FORMAT B:** and then press the Enter key. The following message appears:

   Insert new diskette for drive B:
   and strike ENTER when ready

```
C:\DOS>FORMAT A:
Insert new diskette for drive A:
and strike ENTER when ready

Format complete

    1213952 bytes total disk space
    1213952 bytes available on disk

Format another (Y/N)?
```

Figure 3.7: DOS screen indicating a successfully formatted disk

3. If you have only one disk drive, remove the DOS disk from drive A and replace it with the unformatted disk.

4. Press the Enter key to begin formatting. When the process is completed, you will see the screen shown earlier in Figure 3.7.

5. Press **Y** followed by the Enter key to format another disk. Press **N** followed by the Enter key to end the process.

Keep your computer on for the next exercise.

Making Backup Copies of Disks (DISKCOPY)

The DISKCOPY command allows you to make backup copies of valuable document and software program disks, provided you have at least one floppy-disk drive installed in your computer. This command is a very important DOS feature. If an original disk gets damaged, and it does happen, you will be relieved and grateful that you have an extra copy to fall back on. I make it a habit to back up all my program and data disks, and I highly recommend you do the same. Disk drives have been known to fall apart at just the wrong moment, and it's not a pleasant event.

If your computer has 5¼-inch and 3½-inch floppy disk drives, you will not be able to use DISKCOPY to transfer information between disks. (You can use the DOS command COPY, which you'll learn about in the next section, in this situation.) DISKCOPY will reformat the destination disk to the same format as the source disk. So, if you copy information from a low-density disk onto a high-density disk, the high-density disk will be reformatted to 360K.

You will need two disks for this next exercise—a blank, formatted disk and one with some data recorded on it. Your computer should still be on from the last exercise. Hard-disk users should be in their DOS directory and floppy-disk users should have the DOS disk in drive A.

1. At the DOS prompt, if you have one floppy-disk drive, type

DISKCOPY A: A:

and press Enter. If you have two floppy-disk drives, type

DISKCOPY A: B:

and press the Enter key.

2. For one floppy-disk drive, you will see this message:

    Insert source diskette in drive A:
    Strike any key when ready

    For two floppy-disk drives, you will see this message:

    Insert source diskette in drive A:
    Insert target diskette in drive B:
    Strike any key when ready

3. For a single floppy-disk drive, remove the DOS disk from drive A and replace it with the data disk. Hard-disk users simply place the data disk in drive A. For two floppy-disk drives, remove the DOS disk from drive A and replace it with the data disk and place the blank disk in drive B.

4. Press any key and the copying process begins. In a two-drive system, the data on the disk in drive A is copied onto the blank disk in drive B. In a single-drive system, the information is copied into RAM, where it is stored until it can be copied on the blank disk. After this data is transferred into RAM, you will see the message

    Insert target diskette in drive A:
    Strike any key when ready

5. Remove the data disk from drive A and replace it with the blank disk. Press any key to copy the data from RAM onto the disk. This process may have to be repeated more than once if your RAM is too small to store the entire contents of the source disk. Just follow the screen prompts that tell you when to change disks.

6. After the data disk is fully copied, you will see the message

    Copy another (Y/N)?

7. Press **N** followed by the Enter key to terminate the process or **Y** followed by the Enter key to copy another disk.

Copying Files (COPY)

If you have a hard-disk system, you need a way to copy data stored on the hard disk onto floppy disks and vice-versa. This is especially important for making backup copies of valuable document files. (If you have a dual floppy-disk computer, you also can copy data from a disk in drive A to a disk in drive B, and vice-versa.) For this procedure, DOS provides you with the File Copying command (COPY).

Copying All Files from a Floppy to the Hard Disk

In order to copy data from a floppy disk onto the hard disk, you first must determine which directory you want the information copied to and then use the CD command to change to that directory. When you have completed this step, you can then begin the transfer process. Let's use the asterisk wildcard (*) to copy all the files onto the hard disk.

1. Place the floppy disk containing the information to be copied to the hard disk into drive A and close the latch.

2. At the C>, in the correct directory, type **COPY A:*.*** and press the Enter key.

All the files will be copied from the disk in drive A into the selected directory on drive C.

Be exact when typing these commands, and make sure you know where the files are being copied to—they can end up in some pretty strange places.

Copying One File from a Floppy to the Hard Disk

To copy a single file from a floppy disk onto the hard disk, you type the name of the file after the COPY command. Be sure to use the exact spelling of the file name, including the extension.

1. Use the CD command to change to the directory on the hard disk where you want the file to be copied.

2. At the C>, in the correct directory, type

   COPY A:*FILENAME.EXT*

   followed by the Enter key.

The file called FILENAME.EXT will be read off the disk in drive A and then copied into the hard disk directory.

Copying a File from the Hard Disk to a Floppy Disk

The COPY command is also used to copy files from the hard disk onto a floppy disk. Let's see how it's done. Choose a file on your hard disk to copy. (Use the DIR command to see the files in a directory if you need the exact name of a file.)

1. Use the CD command to move to the directory on the hard disk where the file to be copied is located.

2. At the C>, type **COPY** *FILENAME.EXT* **A:** and press the Enter key.

This tells the computer to copy the file called FILENAME.EXT from the current directory onto the disk in drive A.

Copying All Directory Files to a Floppy

You can use the asterisk wildcard (*) if you want to copy all the files in a hard-disk directory onto a floppy disk. Before you attempt to do this, make sure you have enough room on the floppy disk to store the files. Use the DIR command to display a list of all the files in your chosen directory. You will see the size (in bytes) of each file. Total these file sizes to get an idea of how much space you have left on your disk. A double-density floppy disk holds approximately 360,000 bytes; a high-density floppy disk holds approximately 1,200,000 bytes.

1. Use the CD command to move to the directory where the files are located.

2. At the C>, type **COPY *.* A:** and press the Enter key. Every file in the current directory will now be copied onto the disk in drive A, if there's enough room.

*T*ips on Using DOS Commands

Remember, always think in terms of location when using DOS commands. Be exact in your descriptions when you tell DOS what to do and where to do it. The next section, "Locating and Retrieving Files in DOS," tells you what a path is. This will help you tell the computer exactly where to look for, copy to, or delete a file.

When you type a DOS command, try to translate the command into a logical sentence. For instance,

DEL A:*.*

would translate something like this: "Delete, *from* drive A, *all* the files." The command

COPY C:\PAYROLL*.* A:

would translate as "Copy *from* drive C, *from* the PAYROLL directory, *all* the files, *to* drive A." This command would be similar to telling your assistant to go to the file cabinet labeled C, look in the PAYROLL file drawer, make a copy of all the files, and then place the copies in the file cabinet labeled A.

*L*ocating and Retrieving Files in DOS

Now that you know how to name files and organize them into directories, you need a method for finding these files when you need them. I spoke earlier of the importance of thinking in terms of location when trying to visualize where your documents are stored. Experienced computer operators often use the term *path*. In ordinary language, a path is a route or line of travel from one location to another, and the word has the same meaning in computer language. In order to find and retrieve a file, you must tell the computer on which disk and in which directory the file is stored. You must tell the computer the exact path to the file's location. You have to be precise in your description of the file's location, however, or the computer won't be able to find it. If you make an error, you'll receive a message on your screen saying that the file can't be found.

For example, suppose you have a file named ANTITRST.DOC stored in the GOVMENT directory on drive C of your hard disk. The correct way to tell the computer which path to look along to find this file is

C:\GOVMENT\ANTITRST.DOC

A translation of this path would read like this: "Look on drive C, in the GOVMENT directory, for the ANTITRST.DOC file."

*S*ummary

In this chapter you learned the importance of organizing the information stored on storage disks along the lines of a conventional office filing system. The root directory is the file cabinet, directories are the file drawers, subdirectories are file folders, and files are your documents. Carefully follow the rules for naming directories and files. Think in terms of location when you tell the computer to move from one directory to another, and remember, when you type instructions, to be exact or nothing will happen.

You've also been introduced to DOS commands. You've learned how to create, remove, and move between directories and disk drives, delete and copy files, generate directory lists, and format new storage disks. These commands will allow you to do all the basic tasks necessary to create and maintain an efficient file organization system.

Don't be afraid to ask your supervisor and more experienced co-workers to show you what they know. They may know some more advanced ways of using DOS commands that could help to speed up your work. Always ask questions when things don't operate as they should. The person next to you might have had the same problem last week. As you gain more experience working with your computer, you will learn that there are many ways to do the same task. It's only a matter of time and investigation until you become an expert.

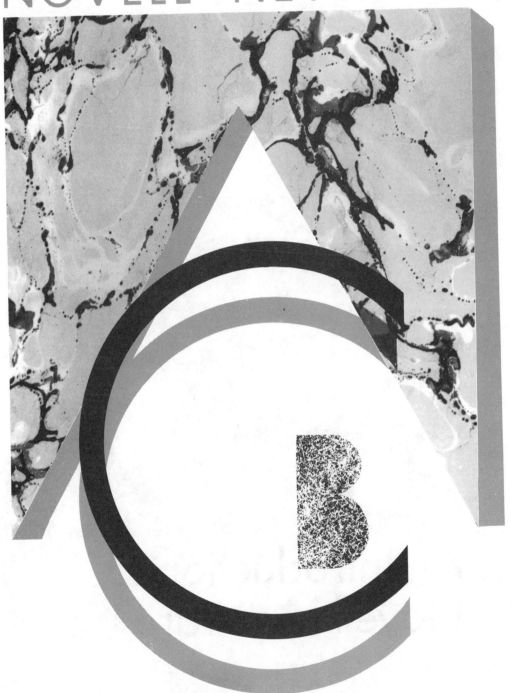

An Introduction to Novell NetWare

If you are new to computers, you will soon discover, as so many others have, that the PC (personal computer), with its own disk operating system (DOS), data processing programs, and self-storage capability, can be used to create, edit, save, and print documents quickly and efficiently. An amazing variety of software programs exists today that can take care of any business need from word processing to aerospace engineering. The type of computer used in these applications, often referred to as a stand-alone computer, has a major limitation, however: it cannot directly share information and resources with other computers.

For example, it frequently happens that more than one individual must edit the same spreadsheet or database. Sharing this document is difficult if it is stored on a stand-alone computer and therefore not easily available to another user. A great deal of time and energy is needed to make copies of data disks to share with others. Also, many businesses cannot afford to provide every computer with an expensive peripheral device like a laser printer. You can imagine the scheduling difficulties in trying to coordinate several print jobs on the only laser printer in the office. These are just two examples of how the stand-alone computer is severely handicapped when it comes to integrated operations between multiple users.

In order to improve efficiency and streamline daily office operations, your computer has been connected to a Novell NetWare local area network, commonly known as a LAN. A NetWare LAN provides three major benefits. First, it permits employees to take maximum advantage of limited computer hardware resources such as printers, fax boards, hard-disk storage facilities, and modems. The second LAN benefit is the shared access by every computer on the network to data processing applications, including word processors, database managers, spreadsheet programs, and graphics utilities. And last, but not least, a LAN enables improved communications among employees working on the network.

This chapter gives you a general overview of what the Novell NetWare system consists of and what it offers to you, the user, so you can take full advantage of the integrated management services provided by NetWare.

Components of a Novell NetWare Network

Transforming the computer equipment in your office into a LAN requires some additional hardware and software. Let's take a look at the main components commonly found in a Novell NetWare system.

Workstations

A stand-alone PC is known as a *workstation* after it is physically connected into the network and has accessed the network's operating system. Sometimes a workstation is referred to by the more technical name, *node*. The number of workstations in a network varies with the data processing requirements of the company and the number of personal computers that can economically be connected into the network.

If your workstation is configured with floppy- or hard-disk storage devices, you also may work independently of the network (locally). This type of computer may have its own peripherals such as a printer, modem, or mouse. Another type of workstation computer, known as a *diskless workstation* because it has no floppy- or hard-disk drives, will process only programs and data files stored within the network system. Many companies feel there is greater security in a diskless workstation because the users cannot copy important data and application files onto floppy or hard disks for their own use.

LAN workstations are generally placed close to each other. They can be placed in one or more rooms in an office or department or, if necessary, spread out over several floors of a building. You can even connect workstations in separate buildings if they are close enough to each other. With the technology that exists today, there is practically no limit to how large, or spread out, a network can be.

Network Cables

Without computer cables there would be no transfer of information between the different components of the computer system. Every workstation has several cables connected to ports (outlets) on the rear of the CPU. If possible, look behind your CPU; you'll see at least four cables, three of which connect your computer to its power source, monitor, and keyboard.

The fourth cable connects the CPU to the central computer that runs the network. Some workstations may even have additional cables for a printer, mouse, or modem.

CAUTION: To guard against a total network failure, do not touch the cables connected to your computer without adequate supervision from your LAN supervisor.

The network cable is your lifeline to the network resources, and therefore care must be taken so it doesn't become damaged or detached from the CPU. Some networks are wired in such a manner that, should a cable become damaged or disconnected, the entire network becomes disabled. If this happens, none of the workstations can process information over the network until the cable problem is corrected.

*N*etwork Adapters

Network adapters contain microchips designed to communicate with the network operating system. Some adapters are built into the computer. Others are placed into a slot inside the computer, and the network cable is attached to an outlet on the adapter (see Figure 4.1). Without a network adapter your computer would not be able to transmit, receive, or interpret any information processed on the network. Communication between network components would not be possible.

*T*he File Server

The network cable runs from your workstation to a powerful centralized personal computer called a *file server*. The file server acts as a central processing and storage point for network applications such as word processors, database managers, spreadsheet programs, and data files. Shared peripherals, such as printers, are also connected to the file server. For instance, if your company has only one laser printer to share among ten workstations, it can be connected to the file server, making it available to all the workstations on the network.

The file server itself can be used as a workstation in some NetWare systems, but it usually functions only as a central storage and processing facility. A file server has a hard disk with a very large storage capacity. Some systems can have as much as 2G (gigabytes) of storage space. Network applications and network data files are stored on the

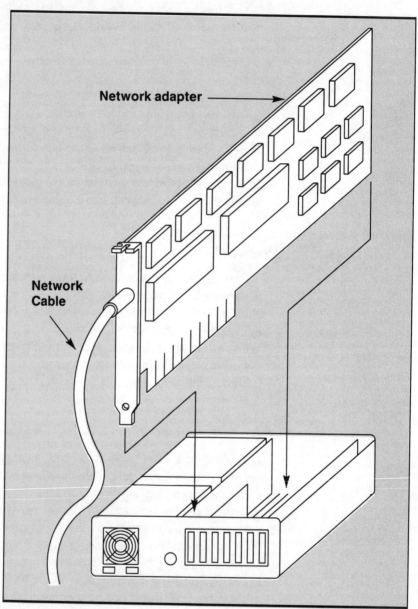

Figure 4.1: *Network adapter and network cable*

file server hard disk, available for use by any operator working in the network. See Figure 4.2 for a diagram of a sample network.

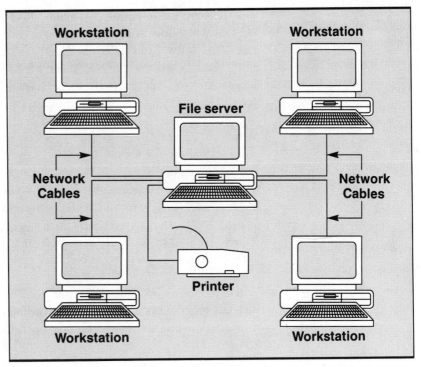

Figure 4.2: *Sample network layout*

*N*etwork Peripherals

In many circumstances, you will not have the luxury of working at a workstation with its own printer, modem, fax board, or even hard disk. You will most likely have to rely on the network peripherals. A NetWare file server can have up to five different printers, in addition to the other items mentioned above, attached to it, available for use by any workstation logged onto the network.

*T*he NetWare Shell: The IPX, and NET2, NET3, or NET4 Files

Installed on the file server is the NetWare operating system that runs the network. It is a completely separate operating system from DOS, which runs your PC. Because the NetWare operating system and DOS are incompatible, you must load special software into your PC that will allow your workstation and the file server to communicate. This software is called the NetWare *shell* and is divided into two parts: the IPX file and the NET2 (or NET3 or NET4) file. You cannot access the file server until these files are loaded into RAM on your PC.

The NET2 (or NET3 or NET4) file differentiates between commands or requests sent to your workstation, which uses DOS, and those sent to the file server, which uses the NetWare operating system. For example, if you type in a request to copy a file or view the files from a local workstation directory on your PC, NET2 directs the request to DOS. If you want to accomplish a task that the network has priority over, such as a request to print on the network printer, the request is directed to the IPX portion of the NetWare shell. The IPX then directs this request to the NetWare operating system located on the file server.

In effect, the IPX and NET2 (or NET3 or NET4) portions of the shell act together as a traffic cop, coordinating and directing requests from the workstation to the proper operating system for action (see Figure 4.3).

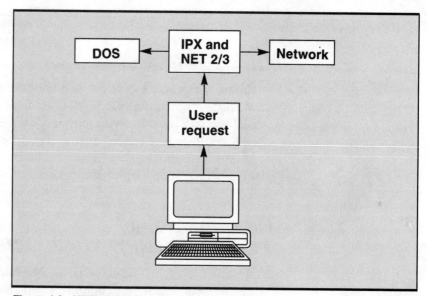

Figure 4.3: *NET2 and IPX traffic control*

*F*ile Server Organization

The NetWare operating system electronically configures the file server so you can run network applications, manipulate network data files, and use networking features. This operating system also allows you to organize your application and data files into an electronic file cabinet similar to the one you learned about in Chapter 3. In order to make NetWare easier to operate, Novell designed the system to work hand in hand with DOS. You use the NetWare operating system to organize information stored on the file server in the same type of directory structure you can create on your local drives using DOS.

As with DOS, a directory can be broken into smaller subdirectories for an even more detailed organization of certain files. See Figure 4.4 for an illustration of a network directory structure.

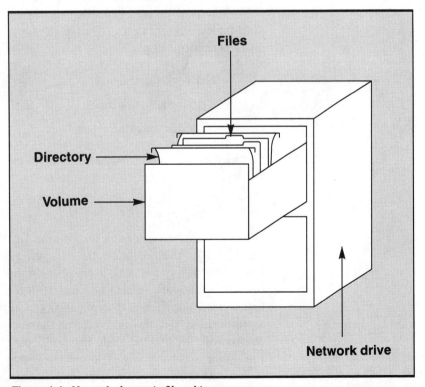

Figure 4.4: *Network electronic file cabinet*

In Chapter 6 you will learn how to create a directory organization system with step-by-step examples.

Who Works on a Network?

Security considerations determine who may operate a workstation on the network. A single file server can store thousands of records and files concerning a company's business transactions, payroll and accounting procedures, personnel records, and so on. It would be improper for all network users to have access to the company personnel files in which confidential information may be contained. The same holds true for payroll files or personal correspondence files. Access to highly sensitive information must be restricted to only those users who have a need to know. NetWare makes it possible to designate these different types of network users, each with their own network access privileges:

- Network supervisors
- Regular network users
- Network operators

Security measures are discussed in detail in Chapters 5-7.

Network Supervisors

Network supervisors are responsible for the efficient operation of the network. They maintain the network system, determine the security rights of any network user, provide guidance and training in the use of the network, create and maintain the primary directory structure for all the files and applications stored on the file server, and monitor the day-to-day activities on the network. Supervisors are also responsible for making daily backup copies of the data stored on the file server in the event the file server crashes.

Take advantage of your supervisor's experience and expertise. There are no dumb questions when it comes to working properly on the network. If you are not sure of a certain procedure, ask your supervisor.

He or she will be grateful for your interest, and your question may prevent inadvertent mistakes that could be harmful to the entire system.

Regular Network Users

Any person who works at a workstation and has access to the network resources in the normal course of a workday is a regular user. As a regular network user you will be able to access any network feature that your security rights will allow. You'll learn more about security rights later.

On many networks you will see a user called Guest. When NetWare is installed, this user is automatically created. The user Guest allows individuals who are not assigned to the network to temporarily enter the network to learn how the network operates, use NetWare utilities, and print documents. The user Guest falls into the category of a regular network user, but with restricted security rights.

Network Operators

A network operator is a regular network user who is given special responsibilities over certain network activities. These special privileges are assigned by the network supervisor. Network operators can provide valuable assistance to the network supervisor by maintaining some of the more routine network operations.

Using DOS Commands on the Network

NetWare makes it easier to work with the network operating system by allowing DOS commands to work on the network. Many DOS commands work the same way on the network as they do on your PC, with some restrictions. NetWare provides its own version of these restricted DOS commands. Some DOS commands will not work on the network at all.

Table 4.1 lists the most common DOS commands, and their network equivalents. More advanced commands are discussed in your supervisor's NetWare documentation.

Table 4.1: Some DOS Commands and their Network Equivalents

DOS Command	Restriction	NetWare equivalent
COPY	Does not allow use of file server and volume names in the path.	NCOPY (COPY can be used)
DIR	Does not allow use of file server and volume names in the path.	NDIR (DIR can be used)
MD	Works only with proper network security rights.	DOS MD is used
RD	Works only with proper network security rights.	DOS RD is used
DEL	Does not allow use of file server and volume names in the path.	DOS DEL is used
DISKCOPY	Cannot use to copy to or from a network drive.	None
FORMAT	Cannot format a network drive.	None

*S*ummary

In this chapter you learned what a NetWare network consists of, who uses it, and what it is used for. NetWare is essentially a management system. With NetWare, your PC assumes a new, more expansive role than that of a stand-alone computer. It becomes an integrated member of a team, able to communicate with other workstations while sharing information, programs, and equipment.

A workstation has its own operating system (DOS), and processes its own files. These files, and the programs used to create them, are stored on a centralized computer called a file server, the control center of the network. The file server uses the NetWare operating system to coordinate all the network activities.

NetWare provides a full-service security system so that restricted information stored on the file server can be protected. A network supervisor, responsible for all aspects of the network, assigns security rights to regular network users and network operators.

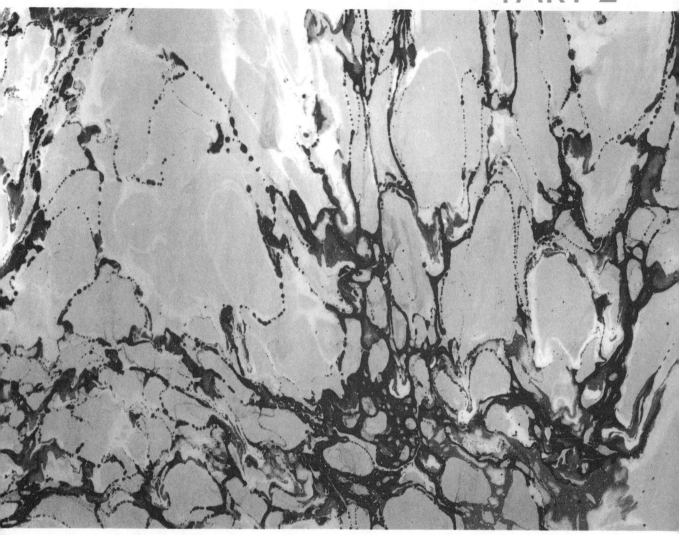

PART 2

Using Novell NetWare
with Your Computer

NOVELL NETWARE

5

Entering the Network

Now that you have a basic idea of what the NetWare network operating system is about, it's time to learn how to use it. For the most part, all the application programs and data files you will work on are stored on the hard disk of the network file server. In order to use the network and begin work, you and your fellow employees must learn how to enter the system, or *log in*. It's not complicated, and there are a couple of ways to go about it, depending on how your supervisor has set up the login procedures.

This chapter will take you step by step through the basic login procedures for gaining access to the NetWare network. Also, once you've logged in to the network, I'll show you how to find out who else is assigned to work on the network with you and how to communicate between workstations.

Usernames, Passwords, and Other Security Considerations

To prevent entry into the network by unauthorized users, you will be assigned both a specific *username* and a *password* by your supervisor. Your username will generally be your first name. If you have the same first name as another employee, a nickname or your last name can be used. Of course, any name can be assigned as a username. It is important to choose a password that would be difficult for someone else to figure out. For example, don't use the name of a close friend or your spouse. If you write the password down, keep it in a safe place and try not to share your password with anybody but the supervisor.

Your supervisor may have you change your password often in order to keep a high level of security. It is almost inevitable, especially in a small office, that passwords become known to fellow workers. When passwords are changed, a higher level of security consciousness is cultivated among workstation users, and overall security is improved.

When you type your password, you will not see it displayed on the screen, and thus roving eyes cannot inadvertently or intentionally see it. The supervisor can limit the number of times someone can attempt to enter an incorrect username and/or password. When this limit is reached, the supervisor will be alerted that an unauthorized attempt has been made to log in to the network, and the workstation will be locked out. If you forget your password, go to your supervisor to straighten out the situation.

Other login restrictions the supervisor may impose include limiting a user's access to the network to specific time periods, assigning specific workstations at which the user may log in, limiting the number of workstations in which a user may concurrently be logged, and disabling a user's network account, which is created by the supervisor.

Be sure to check with your supervisor about the security measures that are in place for your file server. You can become bewildered and frustrated when you suddenly find yourself unable to access the network and can't figure out why.

Logging In to the Network

The supervisor can design your start-up procedure in either of two ways: logging in with an AUTOEXEC.BAT file or from a Remote Reset file, or logging in without an AUTOEXEC.BAT file. As you will soon learn, the first procedure can be performed in three ways: from a custom-designed NetWare menu; with a password only; or with both a password and a Login command.

An AUTOEXEC.BAT file is a file containing a set of instructions that, in this case, automatically logs you in to the network when you boot your system. The file name, AUTOEXEC.BAT, stands for *auto*-matically *exec*ute this *bat*ch of instructions. Normally, your supervisor will create this file for you, but you can create it yourself if you want to. Without this file, you have to enter manually the commands that will allow you to enter the network. A Remote Reset file is a file that is created by the supervisor and is installed on the file server to provide a method of booting diskless workstations. It contains the AUTOEXEC.-BAT file, as well as other files needed for startup.

Before attempting the following exercises, ask your supervisor which of the two login procedures mentioned above has been designed for your workstation, and follow the instructions in the relevant section below.

Also, you'll need to ask your supervisor for this information:

- The name of the network file server

- Your username

- Your password. (If you have not yet been assigned a password, you can still do these exercises, however.)

Logging In with an AUTOEXEC.BAT or Remote Reset File

If you boot your floppy-disk system with a DOS disk from drive A, your supervisor will provide you with a floppy disk that has the AUTOEXEC.BAT file on it. If you boot from a diskless workstation, the Remote Reset file will have been placed on the network file server. If you are a hard-disk user, you may have the AUTOEXEC.BAT file stored on your hard disk. If not, you will have to boot with a floppy disk with AUTOEXEC.BAT on it that your supervisor should provide to you.

There are two ways you can log in with an AUTOEXEC.BAT file. In the first, the AUTOEXEC.BAT file loads up the NetWare shell and executes the Login command, requiring you to enter only your password. In the other, you must manually enter both the Login command and your password. We will cover these two methods with step-by-step instructions.

Turning the Computer On

1. (Skip this step if you have a diskless workstation. Proceed with step 2.) Place the DOS disk that contains the AUTOEXEC.-BAT file in drive A. Hard-disk users may not have to do this step because the AUTOEXEC.BAT file may be stored on the hard disk. However, your supervisor may still have you boot with a floppy disk in drive A.

2. Turn on your computer. If the computer is already on, properly exit any program that might be running and press Ctrl-Alt-Del at the same time. The computer will reboot and read the instructions in the AUTOEXEC.BAT file or Remote Reset file.

You will see a screen that includes the following displays (hard disk users will see C prompts instead):

A>IPX

A>NET3 (NET2 for DOS 2.x, NET4 for DOS 4.0)

A>F:

F>

or

F>LOGIN *file server name/your username*

Enter your password:

Let's pause for a moment so I can tell you what has just happened. The A>IPX indicates that your workstation was booted from the local A drive or the Remote Reset file, and the IPX command was automatically typed in by the AUTOEXEC.BAT file and executed, loading the IPX portion of the shell. Then, AUTOEXEC.BAT automatically typed in *NET3* and that portion of the shell was loaded. The last AUTOEXEC.BAT instruction entered the drive letter *F* in order to change from the local drive to the first network drive, which is indicated by the F> or F>LOGIN *file server name/your username* display. Remember, your first network drive letter may not be F (for instance, a diskless workstation will display an *A>*); don't let it throw you, you are still connected to the network.

Entering the Login Command and Password

If you do not have the Login command in your AUTOEXEC.BAT file (that is, if you just saw *F>* at the end of the last exercise), begin the next exercise at step 1. The Login command (LOGIN) contains the name of your file server and your username, and you will have to enter this information manually. The Login command, file server name, username, and password can be entered in either upper- or lowercase.

For those of you who saw *F> LOGIN* and the "Enter your password:" prompt (refer to the last step in the previous exercise), skip step 1 below and begin with step 2.

1. At the F>, type

   LOGIN *file server name/your username*

   and press the Enter key. The "Enter your password:" prompt appears.

2. At the password prompt, type in your password and press the Enter key, or just press the Enter key if no password has been assigned. You will not see your password displayed on the screen.

At this point, depending on how thoroughly your supervisor has set up your login procedures, you will see one of the following displays on your monitor screen.

- A NetWare customized menu that allows you to select the application programs you normally work with, plus other network options that your supervisor has included in the menu (see Figure 5.1).

- A DOS prompt that corresponds to the first network drive, from which you will have to manually change to the network drive that contains your personal directory or the directory that contains the application programs (see Figure 5.2).

- A DOS prompt that indicates that you have automatically moved to the network drive that contains your personal directory or the directory that contains your application programs (see Figure 5.3).

- A list of all the drive mappings your supervisor has set up for you, followed by the DOS prompt that indicates which drive and directory you are logged on to (see Figure 5.4). You'll learn more about drive mappings and directory organization in Chapter 6.

You are now fully logged in to the network, ready to access the network applications, data files, and share network peripherals with other workstations. Skip the next section and go to "Logging Out of the Network."

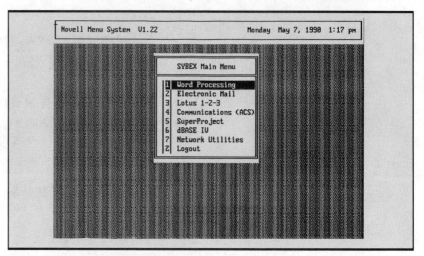

Figure 5.1: *A customized NetWare menu*

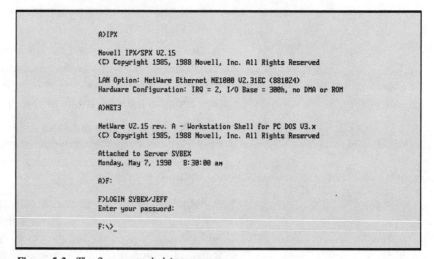

Figure 5.2: *The first network drive prompt*

Logging In without an AUTOEXEC.BAT File

If your supervisor has not installed an AUTOEXEC.BAT file on your DOS disk, whether it be a floppy disk or a hard disk, you must

```
A>IPX

Novell IPX/SPX V2.15
(C) Copyright 1985, 1988 Novell, Inc. All Rights Reserved

LAN Option: NetWare Ethernet NE1000 V2.31EC (881024)
Hardware Configuration: IRQ = 2, I/O Base = 300h, no DMA or ROM

A>NET3

NetWare V2.15 rev. A - Workstation Shell for PC DOS V3.x
(C) Copyright 1985, 1988 Novell, Inc. All Rights Reserved

Attached to Server SYBEX
Monday, May 7, 1990   8:30:00 am

A>F:

F>LOGIN SYBEX/JEFF
Enter your password:

P:\HOME\JEFF>
```

Figure 5.3: *Automatic change to a new network drive*

```
A>NET3

NetWare V2.15 rev. A - Workstation Shell for PC DOS V3.x
(C) Copyright 1985, 1988 Novell, Inc. All Rights Reserved

Attached to Server SYBEX
Monday, May 7, 1990   8:30:00 am

A>F:

F>LOGIN SYBEX/JEFF
Enter your password:

SEARCH1 := Z:.  [SYBEX/SYS:PUBLIC/V3.30]
SEARCH2 := Y:.  [SYBEX/SYS:PUBLIC]
SEARCH3 := X:.  [SYBEX/SYS:PUBLIC/123]
SEARCH4 := W:.  [SYBEX/SYS:PUBLIC/WP]
Drive P := SYBEX/SYS:HOME/JEFF

P:\HOME\JEFF>
```

Figure 5.4: *A sample drive map listing*

type in all the necessary commands to enter the network. You will
need the name of your file server (if there is more than one on your
network), your username, and your password. (Later in this chapter
you'll learn how to create an AUTOEXEC.BAT file to make logging
in easier and faster.)

1. Place the DOS disk in drive A. Hard-disk users may not have to do this step.

2. Turn on your computer. If the computer is already on, properly exit any program that is running and press Ctrl-Alt-Del at the same time. The system will reboot.

3. Respond to the date and time requests either by entering the current date and time or by pressing the Enter key. DOS will load and you will see either an A> or a C> prompt, indicating you are logged on to a local drive.

4. At the DOS prompt, type **IPX** and press the Enter key. The IPX portion of the NetWare shell is loaded.

5. At the DOS prompt, type **NET3** and press the Enter key. (Type **NET2** or **NET4** for DOS 2.x or 4.0.) The NET3 portion of the shell is loaded.

6. At the prompt, type **F:** (if you're using DOS 2.x, type **D:**) and press the Enter key. You have now logged on to the first network drive (F) and are attached to the file server, but you are not yet logged in to the network.

7. At the network prompt, type

   LOGIN *file server name/your username*

   and press the Enter key. You will see a password prompt. (If no password has been assigned, you will not be prompted for a password; you will go directly to the opening screen, as shown in Figures 5.1-5.4.)

8. At the password prompt, type your password and press the Enter key. You will not see the password on the screen. See Figures 5.1 through 5.4 for examples of what you will see on your monitor, depending on how your supervisor has set up the login procedures.

You are now logged in to the network and are ready to access the file server applications, data files, and the network peripherals. Before we go any further, however, let's log *out* of the network.

L*ogging Out of the Network*

You should be able to log out from any location in the network.

1. Properly exit any application you currently have running. Be sure to save the document so you don't lose any important data. If you have a custom menu (see Figure 5.1), you will see that screen; otherwise you'll see a DOS prompt.

2. If your custom menu has a logout option, select it. Otherwise, at the DOS prompt, type **LOGOUT** and press the Enter key. You will see a message similar to this:

   JEFF logged out from server SYBEX connection 1
   Login Time: Monday May 7, 1990   8:30 am
   Logout Time: Monday May 7, 1990   6:30 pm

C*reating Your Own AUTOEXEC.BAT File*

If your supervisor has not created an AUTOEXEC.BAT file that automatically loads the NetWare shell and places you in the network, then you can create your own. This is a very easy procedure, especially if you boot your system from a floppy disk. A hard-disk user will follow a slightly more complicated procedure, so I've presented the steps for creating an AUTOEXEC.BAT file into two sections, one for floppy disks and one for hard disks.

C*reating an AUTOEXEC.BAT File on a Floppy Disk*

You will need the DOS disk that you will use each time you boot your workstation to enter the network. It should contain the IPX file and the NET3 (or NET2 or NET4) file.

1. Place your DOS disk in drive A and turn on your computer. DOS will load into RAM. If your computer is already on, you will need to return to an A> by typing **A:** and pressing the Enter key at any DOS prompt.

2. At the A>, type the following:

   COPY CON AUTOEXEC.BAT

   followed by the Enter key. Now type

   IPX

   and then press the Enter key, and then

   NET3

   followed by the Enter key (type **NET2** or **NET4** if you use DOS 2.x or 4.0.) Finally, type

   PROMPT PG

   followed by the Enter key. (This last line is optional, but recommended. It will display the directory you currently are located in at the DOS prompt.)

3. Now type **F:** (or **D:** if you're using DOS 2.x) and press the Enter key, then type

   LOGIN *file server name/your username*

   Substitute the actual name of your file server and your real username. This will automatically enter your Login command for you. Press Ctrl-Z and then the Enter key.

4. Press Ctrl-Alt-Del at the same time. Your computer will reboot. DOS will read the new AUTOEXEC.BAT file and automatically load the NetWare shell. The Login command will execute automatically, and you will be presented with the password request. If you have not been assigned a password, you will not see this request, but will go directly to the opening screen.

5. Type your password and press the Enter key. You are now logged in to the network.

*C*reating an AUTOEXEC.BAT File on a Hard Disk

You may already have an AUTOEXEC.BAT file stored on your hard disk that accomplishes functions other than entering the network. If this is the case, you probably do not want to lose those instructions, but you will have to add to them in order to be able to enter the network automatically.

1. Turn on your computer. DOS will automatically load into RAM. If your computer is already on, return to a C> by typing **C:** and pressing the Enter key.

2. Type **CD** and press the Enter key. This ensures that you are at the root directory.

3. At the C>, type

   TYPE AUTOEXEC.BAT

   and press the Enter key. The instructions contained in your AUTOEXEC.BAT file are displayed. Write them down exactly as they appear so you can later place the instructions you want to keep into the new AUTOEXEC.BAT file.

4. At the C>, type the following six commands:

   COPY CON AUTOEXEC.BAT

   and press Enter. At this point, you should ask your supervisor if any of the original AUTOEXEC.BAT commands that you copied down in step 3 should be inserted. When you have done so, type in the remaining five commands:

   IPX

   then press Enter.

   NET3

   then press Enter (type **NET2** or **NET4** if you use DOS 2.x or 4.0).

   PROMPT PG

   then press Enter. (This line is optional, but recommended. It will display the directory you currently are located in at the DOS prompt.)

   F:

   and press Enter.

   LOGIN *file server name/your username*

Substitute the actual name of your file server and your real username. This will automatically enter your Login command for you.

5. Press Ctrl-Z, then the Enter key. You return to the DOS prompt.

6. Press Ctrl-Alt-Del at the same time. Your computer will reboot. DOS will read the new AUTOEXEC.BAT file and automatically load the NetWare shell. The Login command will execute automatically, and you will be presented with the password request. If you have not been assigned a password, you will not see this request, but will go directly to the opening screen.

7. Type your password, followed by the Enter key. You are now logged in to the network.

Seeing Who's Who on the Network

Because a network can have a great many workstations set up in a variety of different locations, it is often difficult to keep track of who's working in which department at what workstation. Knowing who is assigned to the network can be important, especially when it comes to internetwork communications and file sharing. NetWare provides the means for you to determine who's who on the network.

In this section you'll learn how to view a complete list of network users, how to find out which users are currently logged in, how to see who belongs to user groups, and how to view some information about yourself. You will also learn how to send a short message from your workstation to one or more other workstations.

To accomplish these network tasks, you will learn how to use NetWare's menu utilities and command line utilities.

A *menu utility* is a small program that provides you with a menu from which you can select different options to perform most network tasks. Menu options are selected by pressing the Up Arrow or the Down Arrow cursor keys to move a highlight to the desired menu item, and then pressing the Enter key. *Command line utilities* are commands that accomplish many of the same tasks as the menu utilities. However, instead of selecting the task from a menu, you type the commands in at a DOS prompt, exactly as you learned to do with DOS commands in Chapter 3.

All of the exercises in this section begin at the DOS prompt. If your start-up procedure provides you with an opening menu, there should be a menu option that will allow you to exit to the DOS prompt and return later to the menu. Select this option from the menu to follow along with the instructions in these exercises. If this exit option is not available on the menu, ask your supervisor for assistance in getting to the DOS prompt to perform the exercises.

*D*isplaying a List of Current Network Users

You can display a list of all users currently logged in to the network with either the SESSION menu or the USERLIST command. Let's look at both methods. Turn on your computer, log in to the network, and follow these steps.

1. At the DOS prompt, type **SESSION** and press the Enter key. The Available Topics menu is displayed (see Figure 5.5).

2. Using the Down Arrow key, move the highlight down to User List and press the Enter key. The Current Users list appears (see Figure 5.6).

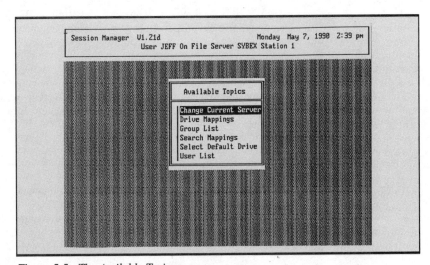

Figure 5.5: *The Available Topics menu*

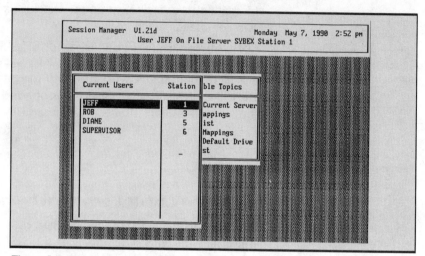

Figure 5.6: The Current Users list

3. To exit SESSION, press Esc twice.

4. At the Exit SESSION box, select Yes and press the Enter key.

Now let's look at the same list by using the USERLIST command. You may find this method is faster than using the SESSION menu utility.

At the DOS prompt, type **USERLIST** and press the Enter key. A list of current users appears on the screen (see Figure 5.7). You are returned to a DOS prompt.

Remember, SESSION and USERLIST display a list of users that are currently logged in. Other users not logged in on the same server are not displayed by either program. To list users from other servers, you must be logged in on that server and type

USERLIST *file server name/*

at the prompt or change servers within SESSION. To view information about all defined users, you must use SYSCON, which is discussed below.

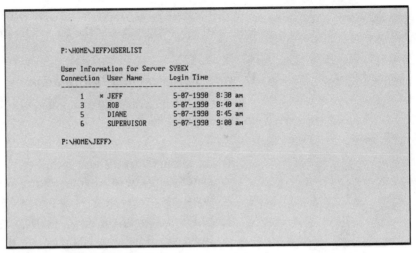

```
P:\HOME\JEFF>USERLIST

User Information for Server SYBEX
Connection  User Name       Login Time
----------  ----------      --------------------
       1    x JEFF          5-07-1990  8:30 am
       3      ROB           5-07-1990  8:40 am
       5      DIANE         5-07-1990  8:45 am
       6      SUPERVISOR    5-07-1990  9:00 am

P:\HOME\JEFF>
```

Figure 5.7: *The USERLIST display*

Displaying User Information with SYSCON

The SYSCON (System Configuration) menu enables you to view accounting change rates, change your password, select another file server, and view information about yourself, other users, and groups. Your personal information includes your full name as it is recorded by the supervisor, which groups you belong to, your security rights, your login script, and more. You can change your own password only if your supervisor hasn't restricted you from doing so. SYSCON also allows you to see the full names of other users assigned to the network and which groups they belong to.

The supervisor can make network operations more efficient and streamline communications by organizing users into groups. For instance, if several people use Lotus 1-2-3 to prepare budgets and financial reports, they could be placed into a group called LOTUS. This grouping makes it possible to send messages to everyone in that group without anyone else on the network receiving them, and to allow that group access to specific files that only the LOTUS group should deal with. It's also quicker and simpler to assign security rights to a group rather than to each member individually.

Security rights are discussed in Chapter 6. The following exercise guides you through a few of the SYSCON menu choices.

Viewing Your Personal Information

In this exercise, you'll take a look at your full name and any groups you belong to.

1. At the network drive prompt, type **SYSCON** and press the Enter key. The Available Topics menu is displayed (see Figure 5.8).

2. Move the highlight down to User Information and press the Enter key. The User Names list is displayed.

3. Move the highlight to your name and press the Enter key. The User Information menu is displayed (see Figure 5.9).

The User Information menu will be used in the next series of steps. We will look at only a few of the items that appear on this menu.

4. Move the highlight to Full Name and press the Enter key. If your supervisor has entered your full name when identifying you as a user, it will appear here.

5. Return to the User Information menu—press Esc.

6. At the User Information menu, move the highlight to Groups Belonged To and press the Enter key. A Groups Belonged To box appears with a complete list of every group you belong to.

7. Return to the User Information menu—press Esc. Keep this menu on your screen for the next exercise.

Changing Your Password

Because of security precautions, the network supervisor will often restrict users from being able to change their own password. If this is not your situation, you can easily change your password to add greater protection for your own data.

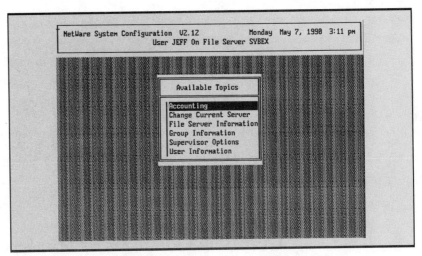

Figure 5.8: *The Available Topics menu*

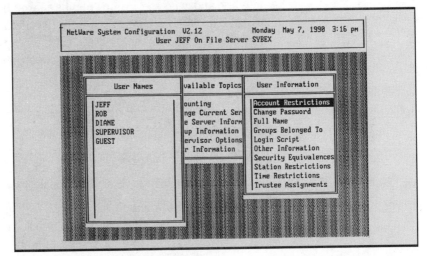

Figure 5.9: *The User Information menu*

1. At the User Information menu (Figure 5.9), move the highlight to Change Password and press the Enter key. This option will not appear on the menu if the supervisor has restricted password changes.

2. Type your old password in the Enter Old Password box and press the Enter key.

3. Type in your new password in the Enter New Password box and press the Enter key.

4. Retype your new password in the Retype New Password box and press the Enter key.

5. To return to the SYSCON Available Topics menu, press the Esc key twice. You should see the menu shown in Figure 5.8.

Keep the Available Topics menu on the screen for the next exercise.

Displaying a List of Group Members

Use this feature when you need to know what groups exist on the network and who the group members are. If you do not belong to a group, you will be able to see only two items, a list of members and their full names. If you are a member of a group, you will be able to see members' full names, the group identifier, a list of members, and the security rights.

1. You should be at the SYSCON Available Topics menu. If not, type **SYSCON** at a DOS prompt and press the Enter key.

2. Move the highlight to Group Information and press the Enter key. The Group Names box appears. All the groups defined for your file server are displayed in this box.

3. Move the highlight to EVERYONE and press the Enter key. Because everyone on the network is a member of the group EVERYONE, you see a complete Group Information menu on the right side of the screen (see Figure 5.10). Take a moment to look at the information provided for each item on the menu. The Group Names box in Figure 5.10 tells you these groups of users are organized according to the applications they use.

4. To exit SYSCON, press Esc three times.

5. At the Exit SYSCON box, move the highlight to Yes and press the Enter key. You are returned to a DOS prompt.

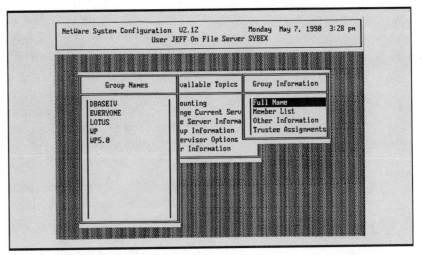

Figure 5.10: *The Group Information menu*

Sending Messages to Network Users

NetWare has an internal message service that allows a user to send short messages, up to 40 characters, to one or more other users or to an entire group. When a workstation receives a message, the message appears on the bottom of the screen in reverse video. There are two ways to send messages: using the SESSION menu utility or the SEND command line utility.

Using the SESSION Menu for Messages

The SESSION menu displays a menu from which you can select the names of the current users and groups assigned to the network to whom you wish to send a message.

1. At the DOS prompt, type **SESSION** and press the Enter key. The SESSION Available Topics menu appears, which you saw in Figure 5.5.

2. Move the highlight to User List and press the Enter key. A list of users currently logged in to the network appears (as seen in Figure 5.6).

3. Move the highlight to your name to send yourself a message and see how it appears on your screen. If you want to send the message to more than one user, move the highlight to each user's name and press the F5 function key to mark each name. After you've selected the person(s) the message will be sent to, press the Enter key. The Available Options menu is displayed.

4. Move the highlight to Send Message and press the Enter key. The Message box appears (see Figure 5.11).

5. Type

   Hello. This is just practice!

6. Press the Enter key. The message is sent. Figure 5.12 shows you what your screen will look like if you sent yourself the message. You will not see this message line on your own screen when you send a message to someone else.

7. To clear a message you've received from the screen, press Ctrl-Enter.

8. To exit SESSION, press Esc three times. The Exit SESSION box appears.

9. Highlight Yes and press the Enter key. You are returned to a DOS prompt.

Now send a message to a group.

1. At the DOS prompt, type **SESSION** and press the Enter key. The Available Topics menu appears.

2. Move the highlight to Group List and press the Enter key.

The groups currently assigned on the network will be displayed. You may choose any group listed, but the group EVERYONE exists on every network. When choosing a group, it's a good idea to select one in which there are no unattended workstations. If you send a message to an unattended workstation that is not set to disable incoming mes-

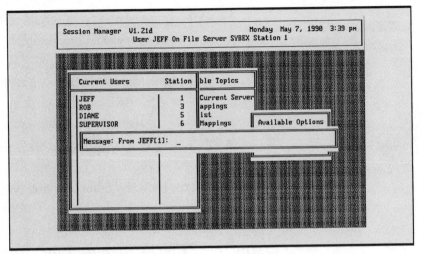

Figure 5.11: *The Message box*

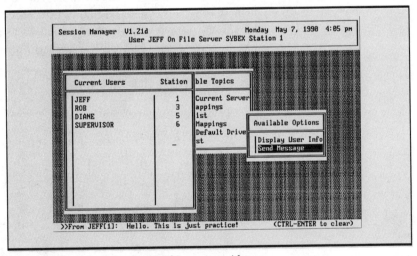

Figure 5.12: *A message displayed in reverse video*

sages, any active operation at the workstation will stop.

3. Move the highlight to the group EVERYONE (or to another group you've selected) and press the Enter key.

4. Type

   Hi everyone! Just practicing.

5. Press the Enter key. The message is sent to every member of the group. If you are a member of the group, you will see the message on your screen.

6. To clear the message from the screen, press Ctrl-Enter.

7. To exit SESSION, press Esc two times. The Exit SESSION box appears.

8. To exit, press the Enter key. You return to a DOS prompt.

Using the SEND Command for Messages

Let's send a message to an individual and a group on the network using the SEND command line utility. This method is faster than using SESSION once you know the format. Determine to whom you would like to send a message; only users currently logged in to the network can receive a message. You can send a message to yourself if you wish. Remember the 40-character limit to the length of a message.

1. At the DOS prompt, type

   SEND "Hi there. Just practicing!" TO *username*

   Substitute the actual username for *username*. Be sure the message is set off by quotation marks.

2. Press the Enter key. The message is sent. You will not see the message on your screen unless you sent the message to yourself.

3. If you received the message, clear the message from the screen by pressing Ctrl and the Enter key. You are returned to the DOS prompt.

Let's send a message to a group. Again, try to select a group that has no unattended workstations. In this example, the message is sent to EVERYONE. Remember, enclose the message in quotation marks.

1. At the DOS prompt, type

   SEND "Hello again!" TO EVERYONE

   If there is another group you wish to send this message to, type the group name in place of EVERYONE.

2. Press the Enter key. The message is sent. If you are a member of the group, the message appears on your screen also.

3. To clear the message from the screen, press Ctrl and the Enter key. You are returned to the DOS prompt.

NetWare's message feature will save a great deal of time and effort when you are sending brief bits of important information to fellow workers, and you can have a lot of fun with it, too. Some networks may have additional, more sophisticated communications packages operating on the network known as *electronic mail* (or E-mail for short). Separate documentation for these programs is supplied by the manufacturer.

Summary

In this chapter you learned about the security requirements for entering a network, how to load the NetWare shell and enter the network, how to identify who else is logged on to the network, and how to communicate with users and groups. Remember, be discreet in dealing with your password, and change it often. There are basically two different ways you can enter the network: automatically with an AUTOEXEC.BAT file or Remote Reset file, or manually. You can also create your own AUTOEXEC.BAT file if your supervisor hasn't done it for you. You also learned to send messages using a few of NetWare's menu and command line utilities.

The next chapter teaches you how to use the network management tools to create and maintain a well-organized directory structure.

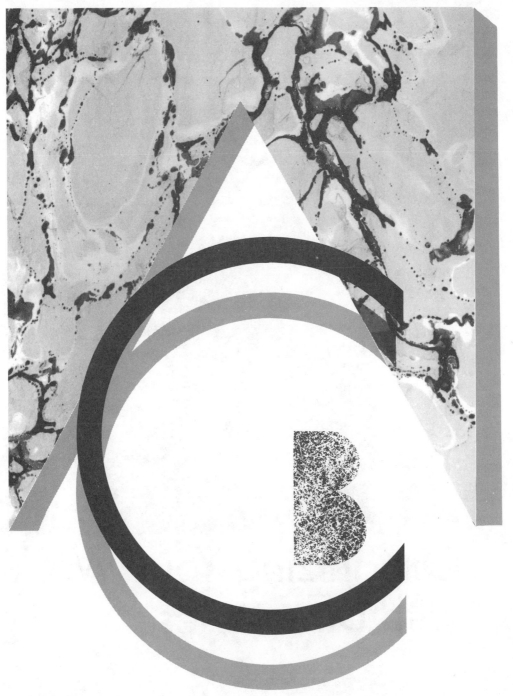

6

Organizing Your Work
with Directories

I stressed the importance of file organization in Chapter 3 when I discussed DOS, the operating system that runs your PC. If you haven't already read it, and if you're new to computers, I recommend you read Chapter 3 before proceeding with this chapter. Organization within the network is equally important. When several users are sharing thousands of files concerning different aspects of a company's operations, it is vital that some systematized way of working with directories be developed. NetWare provides an organizational system patterned after the operating system used by your computer, making it easy to transfer your knowledge of DOS organization to the network.

The network supervisor has primary responsibility for network organization. He or she creates the directory structure that will house the applications and data files that you use in your job. There may be times, however, when you'll need to develop your own limited directory structure.

This chapter introduces you to the security measures that prevent unauthorized access to network directories. You also will learn how to create, rename, delete, and move between directories.

Understanding Directory Security

An understanding of NetWare security is important because security restrictions affect what you can do on the network. The NetWare security system is comprehensive and multilayered, taking into consideration all the possible variations of user and organizational requirements for access to sensitive data.

In Chapter 5 you were introduced to the security procedures that protect unauthorized logins to the network. NetWare also provides an extensive security system that can be used to restrict access to network directories and files. Network users should not have access to every directory or file stored on the file server.

Users are assigned trustee rights. A *trustee* is any user who is given access to the directories and files stored on the network file server. *Trustee rights* are those security options that the supervisor assigns to the trustee.

In addition, the network supervisor can assign security restrictions to specific network directories and subdirectories. These restrictions are imposed by deleting a user's *directory rights* from the directory's *maximum rights mask*. Here's how it works. When a directory is created, all directory rights are on the maximum rights mask and are automatically granted to the user. However, the supervisor can subsequently restrict a user's rights to work in a directory by deleting a directory right from the maximum rights mask. Table 6.1 outlines these security rights. The eight trustee rights and eight directory rights are the same, but each type of right is assigned separately.

Table 6.1: Directory and Trustee Rights

Right	Explanation
Read from existing files (R)	The user can read the contents of a file that has no restrictions placed on it.
Write to existing files (W)	The user can edit the contents of a file that has not been restricted.
Open existing files (O)	The user can retrieve a file.
Create new files (C)	The user can create a new file. The user must have Write (W) rights in order to write data into the file and Open (O) and Read (R) rights to retrieve the file once it has been saved.
Delete existing files (D)	The user can delete files.
Parental (P)	The user can create, rename, and delete directories and subdirectories. The user can also assign access restrictions to limit use of directories by other users.
Search a directory (S)	The user can display a list of all files stored in a directory.
Modify file attributes (M)	The user can rename directories (if Parental (P) rights have been granted) and change the attributes of a file.

A maximum rights mask exists specifically for each directory on the network, so the rights that apply to one directory do not apply to other directories. Changing the directory rights in one directory rights mask will not affect the rights in any other directory.

When a user is given trustee rights to a directory, those rights apply to succeeding subdirectories unless the supervisor assigns new trustee rights at a lower subdirectory level. In order to have access to a directory, the user must have both the trustee right *and* the directory right for that directory. This is known as having *effective rights* for a particular directory. For example, if a user has the trustee right to open an existing file in a particular directory, but the supervisor has deleted the Open right in the maximum rights mask for that same directory, then the user cannot open any file in that directory.

The exercises in the following section show you how to see what trustee, directory, and effective rights you have as a network user.

Viewing Your Trustee Rights

SYSCON is a NetWare menu utility that can be used for displaying a list of your trustee rights in a particular directory. Let's see what trustee rights you have in the network directory that you initially log in to.

1. Log in to the network.

2. At the DOS prompt, type **SYSCON** and press the Enter key. The Available Topics menu appears.

3. Move the highlight to User Information and press the Enter key. The User Names list appears.

4. Move the highlight to your username and press the Enter key. The User Information box appears.

5. Move the highlight to Trustee Assignments and press the Enter key. Your trustee assignments should resemble the list in Figure 6.1. Your rights are represented by the letters in brackets ([]); these letters correspond to those in Table 6.1.

6. To exit SYSCON, press Esc four times. The Exit SYSCON box appears.

7. Press the Enter key. You are returned to the DOS prompt.

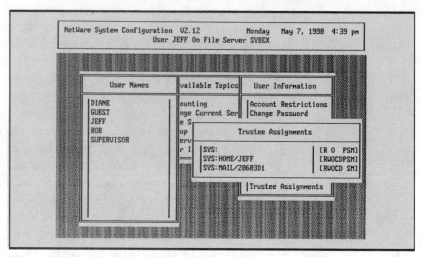

Figure 6.1: *Trustee Assignments list*

Now let's look at the maximum rights mask for that same directory.

*V*iewing a Directory's Maximum Rights Mask

The NetWare menu utility FILER is used to display a list of the rights in a directory's maximum rights mask.

1. Log in to the network.

2. At the DOS prompt, type **FILER** and press the Enter key. The Available Topics menu appears (see Figure 6.2).

3. The *Current Directory Information* option is highlighted. Press the Enter key. The Current Directory Information menu appears (see Figure 6.3).

4. Move the highlight to Maximum Rights Mask and press the Enter key. The Maximum Rights Mask list is displayed (see Figure 6.4).

Compare this list with the Trustee Assigments list you saw in the preceding exercise. If a particular right was not displayed on your list, you do not have that right in the directory listed at the top of your monitor screen.

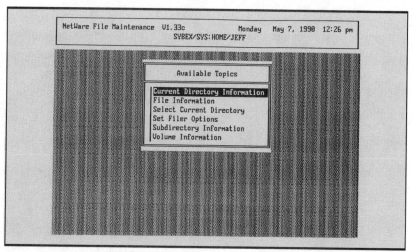

Figure 6.2: *The FILER Available Topics menu*

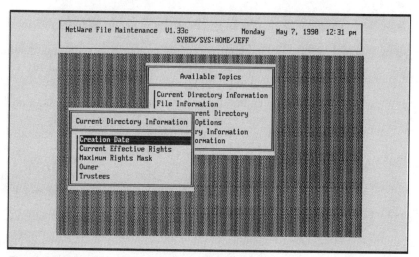

Figure 6.3: *The Current Directory Information menu*

5. To exit FILER, press the Esc key three times.

6. When the Exit Filer box appears, press the Enter key. You are returned to the DOS prompt.

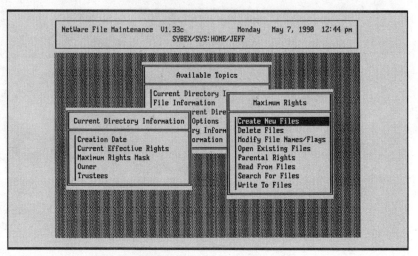

Figure 6.4: The Maximum Rights list

*V*iewing Your Effective Rights

NetWare provides two ways for you to view your effective rights in a particular directory—the FILER utility or the RIGHTS command. Viewing effective rights is a quick way to see whether your trustee rights differ from the maximum rights. The following exercises show you how to use both viewing methods.

1. Log in to the network.

2. At the DOS prompt, type **FILER** and press the Enter key. The Available Topics menu appears.

3. Move the highlight to Current Directory Information and press the Enter key. The Current Directory Information menu appears.

4. Move the highlight to Current Effective Rights and press the Enter key. The Current Effective Rights list appears. It should resemble Figure 6.5.

5. To exit FILER, press the Esc key three times. The Exit Filer box appears.

6. Press the Enter key. You are returned to the DOS prompt.

The RIGHTS command line utility can also be used to see what effective rights you have in a directory. If you like working from the DOS prompt, this is a quick and easy way to determine your effective rights.

1. Log in to the network.

2. At a DOS prompt for the directory you want to know the rights for, type **RIGHTS** and then press the Enter key. A list of rights that resembles Figure 6.6 appears on your screen.

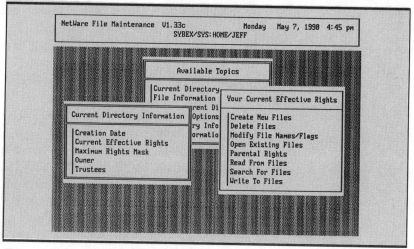

Figure 6.5: *The Current Effective Rights list*

```
P:\HOME\JEFF>RIGHTS
SYBEX/SYS:HOME/JEFF
Your Effective Rights are [RWOCDPSM]:
        You may Read from Files.                    (R)
        You may Write to Files                      (W)
        You may Open existing Files.                (O)
        You may Create new Files.                   (C)
        You may Make new Subdirectories.            (C)
        You may Delete existing Files.              (D)
        You may Erase existing Subdirectories.      (D)
        You may Change Users' Directory Rights.     (P)
        You may Search the Directory.               (S)
        You may Modify File Status Flags.           (M)

        You have ALL RIGHTS to this directory area.

P:\HOME\JEFF>
```

Figure 6.6: *An Effective Rights display using the RIGHTS command*

These are the same rights you saw in Figure 6.5, but they're displayed in a different form.

Establishing a Home Directory

Because every company has specific needs and requirements, directory organizations are unique. Therefore, in order for you to participate in the exercises provided in this chapter, we need to establish a uniform starting point. I will refer to this starting point as your *home directory*. This is where you do all your day-to-day work and store all your files.

Your network supervisor probably has created both a home directory for each network user and a directory called HOME where these user home directories are located. Figure 6.7 shows you an example of such a directory structure.

In the example, the directory HOME has four user home directories attached to it: JEFF, ROB, DIANE, and GUEST. The complete name for Jeff's home directory is \HOME\JEFF, for Rob's home directory it is \HOME\ROB, and so on. Ask your supervisor to draw a directory structure for your network organization so that you can see your place in it. Your login procedure usually places you automatically in your home directory.

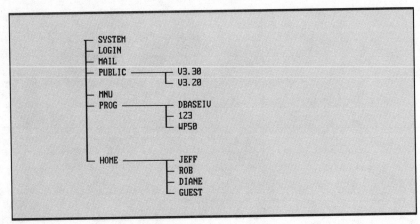

Figure 6.7: A sample HOME directory structure

(In Figure 6.7 you also see several other directories on the network. Four of these—SYSTEM, LOGIN, PUBLIC, and MAIL—are automatically created when the NetWare operating system is installed on the file server. These directories cannot be deleted, and access to the files stored on them is restricted by the supervisor. The MNU and PROG directories are other examples of directories that might be created by the supervisor.)

To do the following exercises, you will need Parental and Modify rights in your home directory so you can create, rename, and delete directories and subdirectories. Check to see if you have these rights in your home directory (see "Viewing Your Effective Rights" earlier in this chapter). If you don't, ask your supervisor to give them to you, or, if this is not possible, to create a directory in which you have Parental and Modify rights in order to do the exercises in this book.

Although your home directory can be assigned any name the supervisor chooses, in this book I will assume your supervisor has followed Novell's suggestion and named the home directory HOME. If your supervisor has used a directory name other than HOME, substitute that name for the name HOME in the following exercises.

Creating Directories

Determine the name of your home directory and make sure you have Parental and Modify rights. Now you are ready to create two subdirectories. You will usually work on the network only in your home directory, so it is important that you organize it well. Break down the work you do into subject areas and create subdirectories based on those subjects. (For example, the following exercise creates LETTERS and REPORTS subdirectories.)

You will use the DOS command MD (Make Directory). These examples will use the home directory for user JEFF.

1. Log in to the network.

2. At the DOS prompt, type

    PROMPT PG

and press by the Enter key. This displays the directory names at the DOS prompt.

3. Move to your home directory. You may need your supervisor's help if you are not automatically logged in to your home directory. Look for a DOS prompt similar to this:

    P:\HOME\JEFF>

    Your home directory name and drive letter will appear where you see P:\HOME\JEFF in this example.

4. At the home directory prompt, type **MD LETTERS** and then press the Enter key. You are returned to your home directory prompt. If you see a screen prompt that says

    Unable to create directory

    either you do not have Parental and Modify rights to your home directory, or a subdirectory with the name LETTERS already exists. In the latter case, alter the name slightly (LTRS or LETTRS, for example) and enter the new name. Use this new name wherever you see LETTERS used in the following exercises.

5. At the home directory prompt, type **MD REPORTS** and press the Enter key. Again, if a subdirectory called REPORTS already exists, make an adjustment to the name and use that name in the following exercises.

6. Type **DIR** and press the Enter key. You will see the two new subdirectories listed in the list of files and other subdirectories that may already exist.

Figure 6.8 shows the new directory structure. Now, when you work in a given subject area, you can move to the relevant subdirectory. For example, if you do word processing often, create a subdirectory where you create all your text documents and always change to that subdirectory before activating your word processor and creating a new document. That way, when you save a newly created document, it will be saved in the word processing subdirectory.

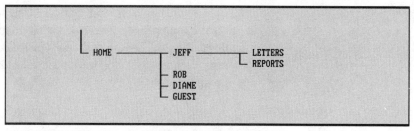

Figure 6.8: *LETTERS and REPORTS subdirectories*

*A*n Overview of Network Drive Mappings

A *drive mapping* is a device that allows you to move quickly and conveniently from one directory to another in the network directory structure. Let's first use the MAP command to take a look at your own drive mappings as they exist on your network.

1. Turn your computer on and log in to the network.

2. At a DOS prompt, type **MAP** and then press the Enter key. A listing of all your drive mappings appears on the screen. (See Figure 6.9 for a sample drive map listing.)

```
Drive  A:    maps to a local disk.
Drive  B:    maps to a local disk.
Drive  C:    maps to a local disk.
Drive  D:    maps to a local disk.
Drive  F: = SYBEX/SYS:LOGIN
Drive  P: = SYBEX/SYS:HOME/JEFF
       -----
SEARCH1:  = Z:. [SYBEX/SYS:PUBLIC/V3.30]
SEARCH2:  = Y:. [SYBEX/SYS:PUBLIC]
SEARCH3:  = X:. [SYBEX/SYS:MNU]
SEARCH4:  = W:. [SYBEX/SYS:PROG/WP]
SEARCH5:  = V:. [SYBEX/SYS:PROG/123]
SEARCH6:  = U:. [SYBEX/SYS:PROG/DBASEIV]
SEARCH7:  = T:. [SYBEX/SYS:HOME/JEFF]
```

Figure 6.9: *A sample drive map listing*

On your listing, you will notice three types of drive mappings: local drive mappings, network drive mappings, and search drive mappings. (If you have a diskless workstation, you will not see any local drive mappings.) It is important to understand how they are used and the differences between them.

Local drive mappings point to the local disk drives located at your workstation (drives A-D in Figure 6.9). When you enter the network, DOS reserves the appropriate number of drive letters to account for all your workstation's floppy- and hard-disk drives. When you type a local drive designator (A:, B:, and so on) at a DOS prompt, you are "mapped," or transferred to that disk drive. The number of local drive mappings you have depends on the version of DOS you are running and the number of disk drives installed on your workstation.

Network drive mappings work differently from local drive mappings in that they do not transfer you to different disk drives; instead, they transfer you to network directories. The network drive mappings in Figure 6.9, drive F and drive P, point to two network directories, SYBEX/SYS:LOGIN and SYBEX/SYS:HOME/JEFF. That is why network drive mappings have an equal sign between the drive letter and the directory name. The F: is the same as, or equals, SYBEX/-SYS:LOGIN. There can be many network drive mappings to many different directories. Your map display may show several such mappings.

Each network user may use the same network drive designator and map it to a different directory. For example, in Figure 6.9 drive P points at SYBEX/SYS:HOME/JEFF. Another network user could have drive P pointing at SYBEX/SYS:PROG/DBASEIV, and still another user could map drive P to SYBEX/SYS:HOME/DIANE/REPORTS. If another user asks you where a particular file is stored, don't tell that person the drive letter; it could be mapped to a different directory on the other person's workstation. Instead, give the actual name of the directory.

Once a network drive has been assigned to a directory, you simply type in that network drive letter at the DOS prompt, press the Enter key, and you're transferred to that directory. You'll get some practice with this in a later exercise.

Search drive mappings tell the network operating system to search designated directories when it can't find a file in the current directory. For example, Figure 6.9 shows you a search drive that reads

SEARCH6: = U:. [SYBEX/SYS:[PROG/DBASEIV]

This means that the sixth search drive mapping is drive U, which points at the directory that contains the dBASE IV program files. Therefore, if you're working in another directory on the network and you want to use the dBASE IV program, you do not have to change directories to PROG/DBASEIV; instead, you simply type the dBASE IV program name at the current directory prompt and press the Enter key. The network operating system initially looks for the dBASE IV program in the current directory. When the file is not found, the system automatically looks through the search directories until it finds the dBASE IV program. You will find all your DOS files stored in a DOS directory with a search drive mapped to it, and therefore you can execute DOS commands from any directory in the network directory structure. The same is true for NetWare's menu utilities, command line utilities, word processing and spreadsheet programs, and so on.

Search drive mappings are usually set up by your supervisor and recorded in the network's system login script. As a user, you may never be called on to create a search drive mapping, but if you need a directory added to the search drives for your workstation, ask your supervisor to create it for you.

An important note: Never change drives from a local or network drive to a search drive. It is possible to change the search drive mapping inadvertently, causing the network operating system to be unable to locate a file when you need it. Changing drives can also cause files to be saved into the wrong directory, making it extremely difficult to find those files the next time you need them.

Notice in Figure 6.9 that the drive mappings begin with the letter A and move forward in the alphabet, while the search drive mappings begin with the letter Z and move backward. When a search drive is created, NetWare automatically assigns these end-of-the-alphabet drive letters to create as large a spread as possible between the two types of drive mappings, thereby reducing the chances of inadvertently changing from a network drive to a search drive.

Creating Network Drive Mappings

Your job may require you to create new subdirectories from time to time. When you do, you may also want to map network drives to them.

Novell provides three ways to map network drives. The first two—using the SESSION or MAP command—create a mapping that is good only for the time you are currently logged in to the network. When you exit the network, the drive mappings are lost and have to be redone the next time you log in. The third method makes a drive mapping permanent. To do this, you must write the mapping into your login script. The next two exercises show you how to use the SESSION and MAP commands. To learn about making a mapping permanent, see the Appendix, "Changing Your Personal Login Script."

Using SESSION to Create a Network Drive Mapping

Let's map a network drive letter to the LETTERS subdirectory you recently created in your home directory. Begin this exercise logged in to the network and located at your home directory.

1. At the DOS prompt, type **SESSION** and press the Enter key. The Available Topics menu appears.

2. Move the highlight to Drive Mappings and press the Enter key. You'll see a listing of your current drive mappings similar to the one in Figure 6.10.

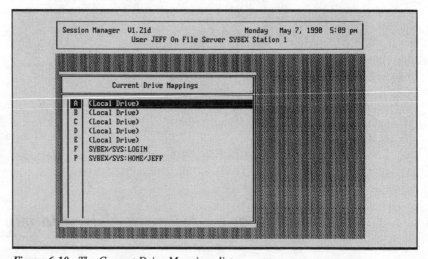

Figure 6.10: *The Current Drive Mappings list*

3. Press the Ins key. The next available drive-mapping letter appears on your screen.

You can delete this drive letter with the Backspace key and enter another available letter if you wish. Let's accept the displayed choice.

4. Press the Enter key. The Select Directory box appears.

5. Press the Ins key. The File Servers/Local Drives list is displayed (see Figure 6.11).

6. Move the highlight to the name of the file server that contains the subdirectory LETTERS. (In this example there is only one file server, SYBEX.) Press the Enter key. SYBEX/ appears at the top of the Select Directory box, and the Available Volumes list is displayed. Again, there is only one available volume in this example, SYS.

7. Move the highlight to the volume that contains the subdirectory LETTERS. Press the Enter key. The volume name appears in the Select Directory box, and the Network Directories list is displayed. In Figure 6.12, you see a list of all the directories on the SYS volume.

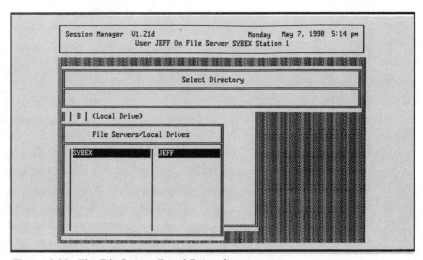

Figure 6.11: *The File Servers/Local Drives list*

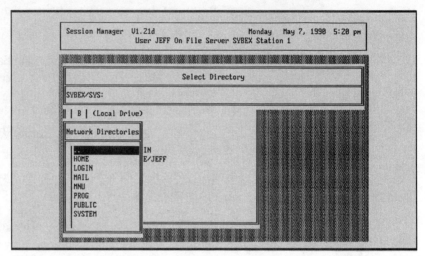

Figure 6.12: *The Network Directories list*

8. Move the highlight to the directory HOME and press the Enter key. The user directories attached to the HOME directory are displayed.

9. Move the highlight to your user directory and press the Enter key. Your directory name appears in the Select Directory box, and the two new subdirectories, LETTERS and REPORTS, appear in the Network Directories box.

10. Move the highlight to LETTERS and press the Enter key. LETTERS appears in the Select Directory box.

The LETTERS directory path has been created. To complete the process you need to save this new drive mapping.

11. Press Esc once and then press the Enter key. The new mapping appears in the Current Drive Mappings box (see Figure 6.13).

12. To exit SESSION, press Esc two times. The Exit SESSION box appears.

13. At the Exit SESSION box, press the Enter key. You are returned to the DOS prompt. If you type **MAP** and press the Enter key, you will see the new drive map list.

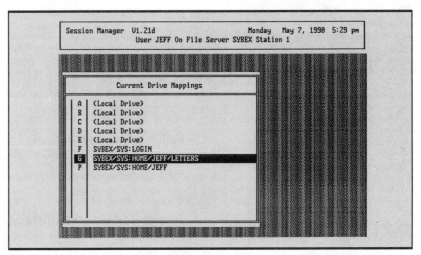

Figure 6.13: *The Current Drive Mappings box*

Using MAP to Create a Network Drive Mapping

In addition to the SESSION menu utility, you can create network drive mappings with the MAP command line utility. MAP is much quicker than SESSION, once you learn the proper format. There are two steps in assigning a drive mapping to a directory. The first is to determine the directory path for the selected directory. The following format is used to describe a network directory path:

file server*/volume name:directory/*subdirectory

For example, SYBEX/SYS:HOME/JEFF is the path for the home directory used in the previous exercises.

The second step is to choose an unassigned network drive letter to assign to the selected directory path. In order to do this, you must know what network drive letters are already taken. With SESSION, NetWare presented you with the next available drive letter. With the MAP command, you must display a list of current drive mappings and choose a drive letter that has not been used for any local, network, or search drive.

In this next exercise, let's create a network drive mapping to the REPORTS subdirectory using the MAP utility.

1. You should be logged in to the network and at a DOS prompt. Type **MAP** and then press the Enter key. The current drive map list is displayed.

2. Select a network drive letter that has not yet been used for a drive mapping or a search drive mapping. We will use the letter G. At the DOS prompt, type

   MAP *n:* = *file server name*/SYS:*home directory*/REPORTS

   Substitute your drive letter, file server name, and home directory name in the appropriate places. The path on your screen should look similar to this:

   MAP G: = SYBEX/SYS:HOME/JEFF/REPORTS

3. At the DOS prompt, type **MAP** and press the Enter key. The new drive mapping appears on your drive map listing.

*M*oving between Directories

There are two methods of moving between directories: selecting a drive mapping that points at the desired directory or using the DOS command CD (Change Directory). Let's use both these options to move between the LETTERS and REPORTS subdirectories you just created.

*C*hanging Directories with Drive Mappings

You learned earlier that when you enter a network drive letter that has been mapped to a particular directory, you will be changed to that location. Let's try it.

1. You should be logged in to the network and located at your home directory. If you do not see your home directory name at the DOS prompt, type

   PROMPT PG

   and press the Enter key.

2. At the DOS prompt, type the network drive letter that you selected to map to the LETTERS subdirectory and press the Enter key. For example, type **G:** and press the Enter key. The DOS prompt indicates the change of location and should resemble this:

G:\HOME\JEFF\LETTERS>

3. Return to your home directory by typing your home directory drive letter at the DOS prompt and pressing Enter. For example, type **P:** and press the Enter key. The DOS prompt indicates you are back in your home directory with a prompt similar to the following:

P:\HOME\JEFF>

It's just that simple to change to a new directory when you've mapped a network drive to that specific location. This is especially helpful when a directory is on another file server or in another volume, or when you have a path that moves through several levels of subdirectories.

*C*hanging Directories with the CD Command

Chances are you won't have every directory and subdirectory mapped to a network drive, and therefore you will occasionally need to use the DOS command CD (Change Directory) to move to a new directory. The CD command works basically the same way on the network operating system as it does with DOS. If you just finished the exercise in the preceding section, you should be in your home directory. Let's change directories to the LETTERS subdirectory with the CD command. After that, you'll move from the LETTERS subdirectory back to the REPORTS subdirectory.

1. If you do not see the name of your home directory at the DOS prompt, type

PROMPT PG

and press the Enter key. Your DOS prompt should resemble P:\HOME\JEFF>.

2. At the DOS prompt, type **CD LETTERS** and press the Enter key. The DOS prompt reads something similar to

   P:\HOME\JEFF\LETTERS>

   You are in the LETTERS subdirectory of your home directory.

Now let's move to the REPORTS subdirectory. Since REPORTS is not attached to the LETTERS subdirectory, you must return to your home directory before changing to the REPORTS subdirectory. This is the same DOS procedure you learned about in Chapter 3 when using your computer in its stand-alone mode. However, NetWare provides a faster way of moving up in the directory structure. By typing CD.. you move up one level in the directory structure. When you type CD... you move up two levels. Let's try it.

1. At the prompt for the LETTERS directory, type **CD..** and press the Enter key. The prompt moves up to the home directory prompt. Now you can change to the REPORTS subdirectory.

2. Type **CD REPORTS**. The prompt changes to the REPORTS subdirectory. Your DOS prompt should be similar to this:

   P:\HOME\JEFF\REPORTS>

Take a moment to practice moving between several different directories, using both your network drive mappings and the DOS CD command. If you obtained a diagram of your network directory structure from your supervisor, target one of the network directories and use the CD command to move there and then return to your home directory.

*R*enaming Directories

As the requirements of your work change, your directory structure also will need to change. A directory name may no longer accurately indicate the kinds of files being stored in it. If you have Parental and Modify rights, you can change the directory name. Be sure to update any drive mappings written in your login script that point at a deleted or renamed directory name (see the Appendix, "Changing Your Personal Login Script").

You can change the name of a directory or subdirectory in two ways: using the FILER menu utility or the NetWare command RENDIR (Rename Directory).

Using FILER to Rename Directories

Let's give the LETTERS subdirectory a new name called MEMOS. Start this exercise from your home directory, since LETTERS is attached to it.

1. At the DOS prompt, type **FILER** and press the Enter key. The Available Topics menu appears.

2. Move the highlight to Subdirectory Information and press the Enter key. The Subdirectories list appears (see Figure 6.14).

3. Find out which function key is the Modify key for your keyboard by pressing the F1 key twice to see the list of key assignments. The Modify key is a special NetWare key used to rename, modify, or edit various menu items. Then press Esc twice to return to the Subdirectories list.

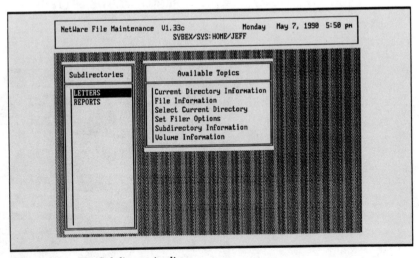

Figure 6.14: The Subdirectories list

4. Press the Modify key. The Edit Directory Name box appears with the LETTERS directory listed (see Figure 6.15).

5. Press the Backspace key until you delete *LETTERS*.

6. Type **MEMOS** and press the Enter key. The LETTERS subdirectory has now been renamed MEMOS.

7. To exit FILER, press Esc twice.

8. At the Exit Filer box, press the Enter key. You are returned to the DOS prompt.

Using the RENDIR Command to Rename Directories

The RENDIR command is a faster method of renaming a directory than FILER. In the last exercise, you changed the LETTERS subdirectory to MEMOS. In this exercise, let's change MEMOS back to LETTERS. When you want to rename a directory, you must be located at the directory to which the directory you want to rename is attached. In this case, MEMO is attached to your home directory, so that is where you want to be.

1. At your home directory prompt, type

    RENDIR MEMOS LETTERS

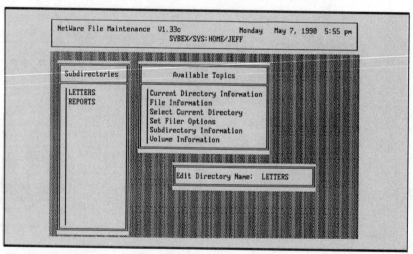

Figure 6.15: The Edit Directory Name box

and then press the Enter key. The MEMOS subdirectory has been renamed LETTERS.

2. To verify the change has been made, type **DIR** and press the Enter key. LETTERS appears on the directory list.

Remember to update any drive mappings to deleted or renamed directories that may be written in your login script. (See the Appendix, "Changing Your Personal Login Script.")

*D*eleting Directories

When a directory or subdirectory is no longer needed to store files, it is good practice to delete it. Deletion keeps the directory structure from becoming cluttered with unnecessary directory names. Be sure to delete the respective drive mappings in your login script when you delete directories.

There are two ways to delete directories: with the FILER menu utility or with the DOS command RD (Remove Directory). Let's look at them both.

*U*sing FILER to Delete Directories

Let's use the FILER menu utility to delete the LETTERS subdirectory. FILER can delete the files and the directory name at the same time, or delete only the files; you'll use FILER to delete the entire directory structure.

1. At your home directory prompt, type **FILER** and press the Enter key. The Available Topics menu appears.

2. Move the highlight to Subdirectory Information and press the Enter key. The Subdirectories list appears.

3. Move the highlight to the LETTERS subdirectory and press the Delete key. The Delete Subdirectory Options box appears (see Figure 6.16).

You are offered two choices: to delete the entire subdirectory structure, which includes all the files and subdirectories within it and the
subdirectory name itself, or to delete only the files.

4. Move the highlight to Delete Entire Subdirectory Structure and
   press the Enter key. The Delete Entire Directory Structure box
   appears (see Figure 6.17).

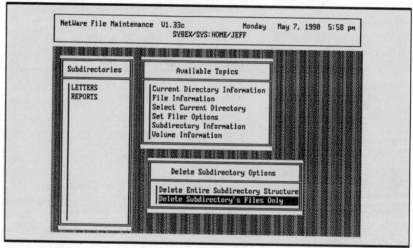

Figure 6.16: *The Delete Subdirectory Options box*

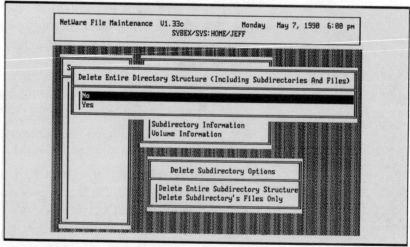

Figure 6.17: *The Delete Entire Directory Structure box*

5. Move the highlight to Yes and press the Enter key. The LET-
   TERS subdirectory disappears from the Subdirectories list.

6. To exit FILER, press Esc until the Exit Filer box appears, then
   press the Enter key. You are returned to the DOS prompt.

Using the RD Command to Delete Directories

To remove a subdirectory with the RD command (Remove Directory), you must be in the directory to which the subdirectory is
attached. Before you can delete a subdirectory with the RD command,
you must delete all the files in that subdirectory and any subdirectories
within it. In this exercise you'll delete the REPORTS subdirectory, so
you should be located in your home directory.

1. At your home directory prompt, type **RD REPORTS** and
   press the Enter key. You are returned to your home directory
   prompt.

2. Type **DIR** and press the Enter key. You will see that the
   RECORDS subdirectory is no longer attached to your home
   directory.

Summary

In this chapter you learned how to create a directory structure
where you can store your network files in an organized manner. You
know how to use SESSION and FILER and several other utilities to
rename, delete, map, and move between directories on the network.

Network directory paths include the name of the file server, the
volume, the directory, and all subsequent subdirectories. It is important you become familiar with the correct format for specifying a network directory path.

Usually you will have the security rights to create directories only
in your home directory. This restriction prevents users from accidentally changing the main directory structure the supervisor has established for the network.

Remember, search drive mappings are there only to provide the network operating system with a method of searching out files that aren't in the directory in which you are currently working. This means you can execute DOS commands, NetWare menu utilities, NetWare command line utilities, and application programs from any directory as long as there is a search drive mapped to the directory that contains the appropriate files. Be careful not to change from network or local drives to search drive mappings; you can inadvertently affect the mapping, making it impossible to access the files in that directory.

Chapter 7 introduces you to network file management. The file server can store thousands of files, and it is important to know how to manage them efficiently. You'll learn how to rename, delete, and make copies of files. I will also discuss the importance of file security and how it affects your ability to access files stored on the file server.

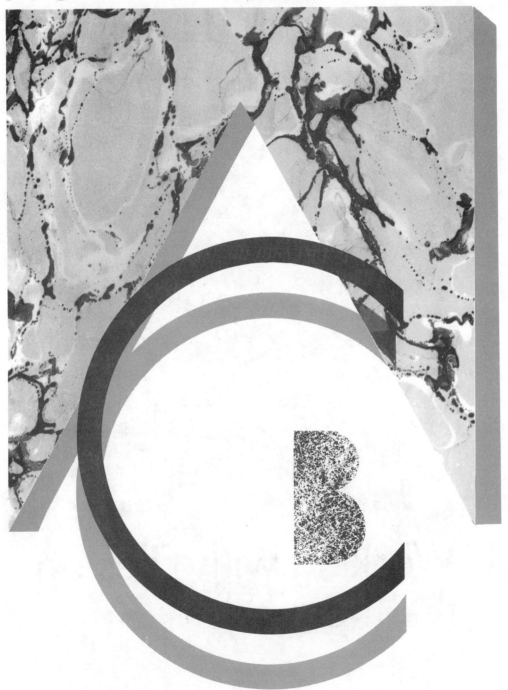

Working with Files on the Network

In Chapter 6 you learned how to work with directories, the file folders of your electronic file cabinet. As time goes by, you and your associates will create hundreds of files, all of which will be stored in these directories. In order to prevent such a large number of files from becoming unmanageable, NetWare provides several file maintenance tools. These tools are similar to the DOS file management tools you learned about in Chapter 3. Many of the NetWare commands are the same as those used by DOS. If you are familiar with DOS, you will find it easy to learn the NetWare system.

In this chapter you will learn how to move files from one location to another, rename files for greater ease of identification, and delete files that are no longer needed. You will also learn about security measures that will prevent files from being edited, deleted, or shared by other users.

Creating and Viewing a Sample File

In the next few exercises you will use the DOS command COPY CON to create an expendable file that you will experiment with. You will also log in to a directory in which you have full trustee and directory security rights. See Chapter 6 for instructions on viewing your effective rights in a directory. Usually, your home directory will give you the rights you need.

Let's create a file called MODIFY in your home directory.

1. Log in to the network and move to your home directory or a directory in which you have full effective rights.

2. At the DOS prompt, type

   COPY CON MODIFY

   and press the Enter key. You are *copy*ing from the *con*sole to the file named *MODIFY*.

   Type

   Changing a file's attributes is important for file security.

   and press the Enter key.

4. Press Ctrl-Z and then the Enter key. You have just created a sample file called MODIFY in your home directory.

To display the information recorded in the file you just created, use the DOS TYPE command.

1. Make sure you are still in the directory where the MODIFY file was created and saved.

2. At the DOS prompt, type **TYPE MODIFY** and press the Enter key. The contents of the file are displayed on the screen.

The TYPE command will work with any text file. Don't use the TYPE command to view program files, however; you won't be able to see anything. A file that is larger than one screen's worth of text will rapidly scroll on and off the screen, making the file difficult to read. To stop the scrolling, hold the Ctrl key down and press the S key simultaneously. When you are ready to resume scrolling, press the S key again while continuing to hold the Ctrl key down. Press the S key to stop and start the scrolling until you have read the entire contents of the file.

Viewing a Directory File List with the NDIR Command

NetWare provides you with its own version of the DOS DIR command, NDIR (Network Directory). NDIR displays file information similar to what DIR provides, but with some added information pertaining to the network environment.

Figure 7.1 shows you an example of a file listing for the HOME directory using the NDIR command. In addition to the normal information—file name, size, and date and time last modified—NDIR gives you the last time the file was accessed, the file attribute flags placed on the file, and the username of the person who created or last modified the file. You also get a list of subdirectories in that directory, including the date and time the subdirectory was created, the maximum rights mask, the effective rights, and the username of the person who created the directory.

```
P:\HOME\JEFF>ndir
SYS:HOME/JEFF
File Name       Size    Last Modified    Accessed Created  Flags      Owner
--------------  ------  ---------------  -------- --------  ---------  ------------
CNTRACTS             9  4-17-90  4:57p   4-17-90 10-10-89 [W-M----] JEFF
RECORDS            567  4-23-90  2:22p   4-23-90  7-17-89 [W-M----] JEFF
RESUME    DOC     4243  4-29-90  2:17p   4-29-90 11-22-89 [W-M----] JEFF


Directory Name Created           Max Rights  Eff Rights Owner
-------------- --------------    ----------  ---------- ------------
ACCOUNTS       5-7-90   1:40p [RWOCDPSM] [RWOCDPSM] JEFF
REPORTS        5-7-90   1:41p [RWOCDPSM] [RWOCDPSM] JEFF
         2 sub-directories found

Total: 3 files using 4819 bytes
Total disk space in use: 16384 bytes (4 blocks)

P:\HOME\JEFF>
```

Figure 7.1: *A NDIR file listing*

With the NDIR command you can display a great deal of information about files and subdirectories for any directory, information that can be helpful in maintaining a well-organized file management program.

Understanding File Security

In addition to the comprehensive security measures you learned about in Chapters 5 and 6, NetWare also provides a file attribute security system to prevent an individual file from being edited by or shared with other network users. (You'll learn about file attributes in a moment.) It is important to protect valuable files from being accidentally changed or deleted. You can imagine the chaos that would result if, for example, a 50,000-item database was innocently deleted by a network user. Files of this nature are usually restricted to reading only; no editing of them is allowed. Certain program files, such as DOS commands, will also often be restricted from being written to in order to protect the integrity of the program.

Defining File-Security Attributes

Four basic file attributes affect the security of a network file. These security attributes are

Read/Write	Any user with the appropriate trustee rights can read from, write to, rename, or delete the file.
Read Only	Any user with the appropriate trustee rights can read the file. The user cannot edit, rename, or delete the file.
Shareable	These files may be read by more than one user at the same time. Large data files are often marked as Shareable.
Non-shareable	These files may be accessed by only one user at a time.

When a file is initially created, it is marked as Read/Write and Non-shareable. Any user can edit, rename, or delete the file. You will have to change the file attributes if you want to restrict access to the file after it is created.

File attributes take precedence over trustee and directory rights. A user may have full effective rights in a directory, but if a particular file has Non-shareable, Read Only attributes, that person cannot access the file.

*W*orking with File Attributes

NetWare provides two methods of modifying a file's attributes: the FILER menu utility and the FLAG command line utility. When you mark a file with a particular attribute, it is often referred to as being *flagged*.

Displaying a List of Files and Their Attributes

The FILER menu utility can be used to display a list of files in a particular directory. You can then select a file from the directory list and display the file's attributes, a helpful technique when you are not sure what attributes are assigned to a particular file. Let's take a look at the file attributes for the file MODIFY that you created in the first exercise.

1. At the DOS prompt, type **FILER** and press the Enter key. The Available Topics menu appears.

2. Move the highlight to File Information and press the Enter key. A list of files stored in the directory is displayed.

3. Move the highlight to MODIFY and press the Enter key. The File Information list is displayed.

4. Move the highlight to Attributes and press the Enter key. The File Attributes list appears (see Figure 7.2).

The Modified Since Last Backup entry means the file has been edited since the last time the file was backed up by the supervisor and therefore there is no backup copy of this file. No other attributes are listed, indicating that the file can be edited, but cannot be shared.

Keep the File Attributes list on the screen and proceed with the next exercise.

Using FILER to Change File Attributes

Now that you know how to display a list of attributes for a particular file, let's use the FILER menu utility to change the attributes for the file MODIFY. Right now the attributes allow the file to be edited by others. Let's restrict the file so it can only be read, not edited.

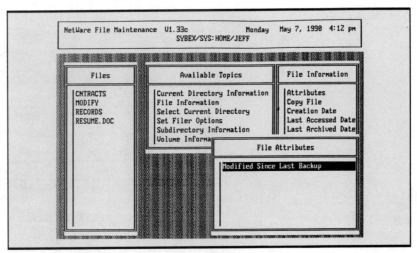

Figure 7.2: *The File Attributes list for MODIFY*

1. With the File Attributes list on the screen from the last exercise, press the Ins key. The Other File Attributes list appears at the left of your screen (see Figure 7.3).

This is a list of attributes you can assign to a file. The Hidden File, Indexed, and System File attributes are beyond the level of this book and will not be covered. All files are non-shareable and can be read and written to, so the Read/Write and Non-shareable attributes do not appear on this list.

2. Move the highlight to Read Only and press the Enter key. The Read Only attribute is placed in the File Attributes list, and the file may no longer be edited, renamed, or deleted.

Now restore the Read/Write attribute.

3. Place the highlight on Read Only and press the Delete (Del) key. The Remove File Attribute box appears (see Figure 7.4).

4. With the highlight on Yes, press the Enter key. The file has been restored to its original Read/Write status, and you may now edit, rename, or delete the file.

5. To exit from FILER, press the Esc key four times.

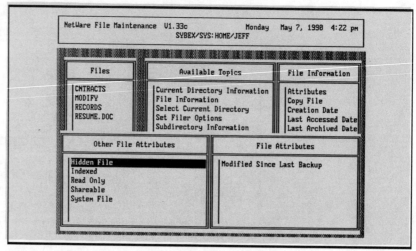

Figure 7.3: The Other File Attributes list

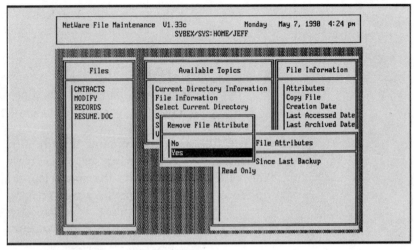

Figure 7.4: *The Remove File Attribute box*

6. At the Exit Filer box, press the Enter key. You are returned to the DOS prompt.

Using FLAG to View and Change File Attributes

The FLAG command line utility may also be used to list and change the file attributes of a file. Let's list the file attributes of the file MODIFY and change the attributes from Read/Write to Read Only.

1. At the DOS prompt, type **FLAG MODIFY** and press the Enter key. The attributes for the file MODIFY are displayed on your screen. They should read

   MODIFY   Non-shareable   Read/Write

2. To change the attribute to Read Only, type

   FLAG MODIFY RO

   (for Read Only) and press the Enter key. A modified attributes list appears on your screen. The file MODIFY is now flagged

   MODIFY   Non-shareable   ReadOnly

Let's change the attribute back to Read/Write.

3. At the DOS prompt, type

    FLAG MODIFY RW

    (for Read/Write) and press the Enter key. Once again, the display shows the Non-shareable and Read/Write attributes.

The following list contains the file attributes that you will most often use for security purposes. When typing in the FLAG command at the DOS prompt, use the abbreviation after the file name to tell NetWare which attribute you want to flag.

Attribute	Abbreviation
Read Only	RO
Read/Write	RW
Shareable	S
Non-shareable	NS

Renaming Files

It is occasionally necessary to change the name of a file to reflect the file's contents more accurately or to aid in file organization. For example, suppose you want to create some additional sample files and organize them into a group with similar names, such as SAMPLE1, SAMPLE2, SAMPLE3, and so on. You also want to include the file MODIFY that you created in the first exercise. You have to change the name of MODIFY to fit in with the new naming scheme.

You can use either the FILER menu utility or the DOS command REN (Rename) to change the name of a file.

Using FILER to Rename a File

In this exercise, let's change the name of the sample file MODIFY to SAMPLE1 using the FILER menu utility. You may use any file you wish for these exercises if you have not created this file. (See "Creating and Viewing a Sample File" in this chapter.)

1. If you aren't logged in to the network, log in and move to the directory that has the sample file MODIFY; this should be your home directory.

2. At the DOS prompt, type **FILER** and press the Enter key. The Available Topics menu appears.

3. Move the highlight to File Information and press the Enter key. The Files list appears.

4. Move the highlight to MODIFY and press F3, the Modify key. (If F3 doesn't work, press F1 twice to see which key is the Modify key for your keyboard.) The Edit File Name box appears with the MODIFY file listed (see Figure 7.5).

5. Backspace until the MODIFY file name is deleted and type **SAMPLE1** and press the Enter key. MODIFY is now called SAMPLE1 and is placed in the Files list.

6. To exit FILER, press the Esc key twice.

7. At the Exit Filer box, press the Enter key. You are returned to the DOS prompt.

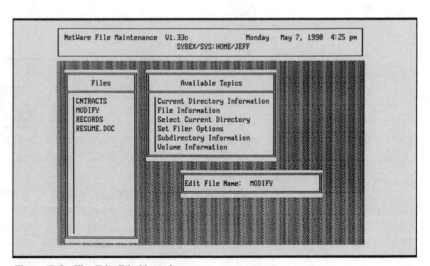

Figure 7.5: *The Edit File Name box*

8. Type

NDIR SAMPLE1

and press the Enter key to check the directory. The directory list shows the file SAMPLE1.

Using the REN Command to Rename a File

Using the REN (Rename) command is a quick way to change a file's name from the DOS prompt. Let's change SAMPLE1 to SAMPLE2.

1. At the DOS prompt for the directory that has the SAMPLE1 file, type

REN SAMPLE1 SAMPLE2

and press the Enter key. The file name has been changed from SAMPLE1 to SAMPLE2.

2. Type

NDIR SAMPLE2

and press the Enter key to check the directory. The directory list shows the file SAMPLE2.

Copying Files

Being able to copy files from one location to another is helpful in keeping a well-organized and uncluttered directory structure. With NetWare, you can copy files from one directory to another on the network, from a network directory to a local disk drive, from one local disk drive to another local disk drive, and from a local disk drive to a directory on the network.

To copy a file, you need to be able to specify accurately the location of the originating file (the source directory) and the destination directory. Having a good understanding of paths also is necessary. When the computer looks for a network file, it looks first on the file server, then in the correct volume, then in a directory, and then, if there are any, it looks in subsequent subdirectories. If you expect the computer to find a file in a certain directory and copy it to another directory, you must be able to describe the two locations exactly.

You need Read, Open, and Search rights in the source directory and Open, Create, Write, and Delete rights in the destination directory. If you have trouble copying files into another directory outside your home directory, you may not have the appropriate rights.

There are two ways to copy files on the network: with the FILER menu utility and the NCOPY command line utility.

*U*sing FILER to Copy Files

FILER simplifies the copy procedure if you aren't sure of the exact directory path where you want to copy a file. In this exercise, we'll create two new subdirectories, NEWPARTS and OLDPARTS, in your home directory structure and copy the file SAMPLE2 between them.

1. Log in to the network, if you aren't already in, and move to your home directory.

2. At the DOS prompt, type **MD NEWPARTS** and press the Enter key.

3. Now type **MD OLDPARTS** and press the Enter key. You have created two new subdirectories.

4. At the DOS prompt, type **FILER** and press the Enter key. The Available Topics menu appears.

5. Move the highlight to File Information and press the Enter key. The Files list appears.

6. Move the highlight to the file SAMPLE2 and press the Enter key. The File Information box appears.

7. Move the highlight to Copy File and press the Enter key. The Destination Directory box appears (see Figure 7.6).

You'll copy SAMPLE2 to the NEWPARTS directory.

8. Type in the full directory path for the destination directory; for example

   SYBEX/SYS:HOME/JEFF/NEWPARTS

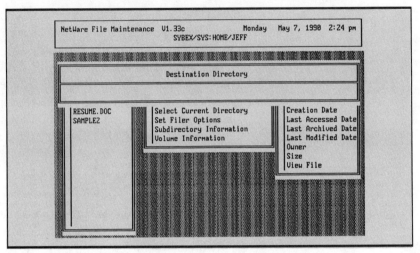

Figure 7.6: The Destination Directory box

and press the Enter key. (If you don't know the directory path, skip to step 10 and let FILER help you.) The Destination File Name box, with the file SAMPLE2 entered, appears (see Figure 7.7). (At this point, you could delete the file name and type in a new name, but for this exercise, don't change the name of SAMPLE2.) If you entered the path incorrectly, you will see this prompt:

Specified Directory Does Not Exist
< Press ESCAPE to continue>

Just press the Esc key and reenter the path.

There's a handy shortcut you can use when typing in the directory path for the destination drive. If the directory is mapped to a drive letter, you can just type in the drive letter instead of the entire path. For example, if you have the NEWPARTS subdirectory mapped to drive L, you simply type in **L:** in the Destination Directory box— another nice reason to map drives to directories.

9. With SAMPLE2 in the Destination File Name box, press the Enter key. The file is copied to the NEWPARTS subdirectory. Skip steps 10 through 20 and go to step 21 and exit FILER. Steps 10-20 are for those who do not know the directory path.

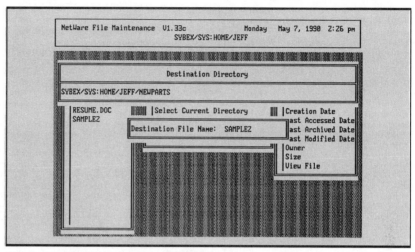

Figure 7.7: *The Destination File Name box*

10. If you do not know the directory path, the Destination Directory box will be blank. Press the Insert (Ins) key. The File Servers/Local Drives list is displayed. If the file server you want does *not* appear on the File Servers/Local Drives List, then you are not attached to it; you'll need to attach to a new file server. Skip step 11 and go to step 12.

11. Move the highlight to the file server you want (if you have more than one) and press the Enter key. The file server name appears in the Destination Directory box, and the Volumes list appears on the screen (see Figure 7.8). Skip steps 12 through 15 (these steps are for those who need to attach to a different file server) and go to step 16.

12. To attach to a different file server, press Ins. The Other File Servers list is displayed.

13. Move the highlight to the server you want and press the Enter key. The New User Name box appears.

14. Type in your username and press the Enter key. The Password box appears if a password is required to access the server.

15. Type in the password (if needed) and press the Enter key. You are attached to the new file server, and its name is added to

the File Servers/Local Drives list. Highlight the new server name and press Enter. The Volumes list appears.

16. If the Volumes list is not displayed, be sure no volume is listed in the Destination Directory box and press Ins. Move the highlight to the volume you want and press the Enter key. The volume name appears in the Destination Directory box. The Network Directories list appears (see Figure 7.9).

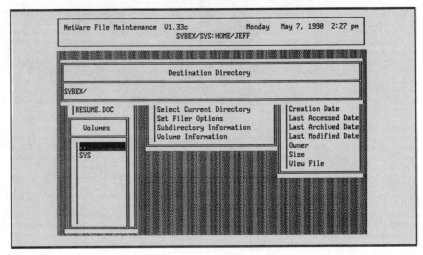

Figure 7.8: *The Volumes list*

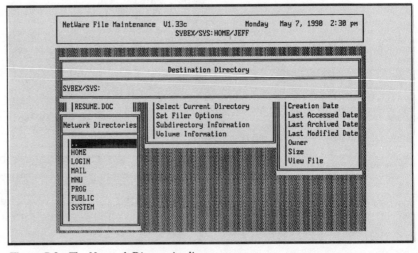

Figure 7.9: *The Network Directories list*

17. Move the highlight to the directory to which you want to copy the file (your home directory in this case) and press the Enter key. The directory is added to the destination directory path. Repeat this step two more times to select the subdirectories leading to the NEWPARTS subdirectory.

18. When the directory path is completed, press the Esc key. The Destination Directory box now has a full path name for the NEWPARTS subdirectory.

19. Press the Enter key. The Destination File name box appears with SAMPLE2 entered. You could delete the name of the file to be copied and type in a new name, but for the purposes of this exercise do not do so.

20. Press Enter. The file is copied to the destination directory.

21. To exit FILER, press Esc three times.

22. At the Exit Filer box, press the Enter key. You are returned to a DOS prompt.

If you try to copy a file into a directory that has a file with the same name already stored there, you will see the box and the prompt shown in the lower half of Figure 7.10.

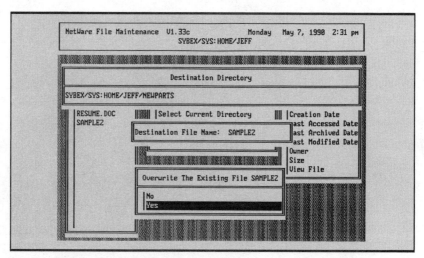

Figure 7.10: *The Overwrite The Existing File box*

If you want to see if the file SAMPLE2 was copied to the subdirectory NEWPARTS, change directories to NEWPARTS and use the NDIR command to list the files.

You can see that knowing the destination directory path shortens the process considerably when you are copying files with FILER. Ask your supervisor to provide you with a directory tree (see Figure 7.11) for your network. It will be a tremendous aid in specifying the correct path to any directory.

Using the NCOPY Command to Copy Files

The NCOPY command line utility is a quick way of copying files from the DOS prompt. Again, you must be able to describe the source location of the file to be copied and the destination location to which it is to be copied. For example, if you are in your home directory and you want to copy the file SAMPLE2, located in the NEWPARTS subdirectory, to the OLDPARTS subdirectory, you would type at the DOS prompt

```
NCOPY SYS:HOME/JEFF/NEWPARTS/SAMPLE2 TO
SYS:HOME/JEFF/OLDPARTS
```

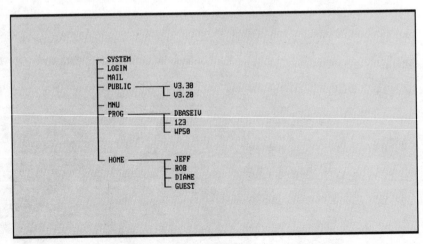

Figure 7.11: A sample directory tree

Both the source directory and the destination directory have been described accurately. However, it's time consuming to type full directory paths for both the source and destination directories, and fortunately there are a couple of shortcuts.

If you are in the directory that contains the file to be copied, you do not need to specify the entire source path. For example, if you are in the NEWPARTS subdirectory and want to copy SAMPLE2 to the OLDPARTS subdirectory, you would type

NCOPY SAMPLE2 TO SYS:HOME/JEFF/OLDPARTS

There is less to type if you move to the source directory before copying files from it.

Another shortcut for copying files is to use drive mappings. If SYS:HOME/JEFF/OLDPARTS was mapped to drive M, for example, and you were located in the NEWPARTS subdirectory, you would type

NCOPY SAMPLE2 TO M:

That would be it. The computer finds SAMPLE2 because you are already located in the NEWPARTS subdirectory and copies it to drive M, which is equivalent to the path to OLDPARTS.

You can use NCOPY to copy files between the network file server and the local disk drives if you use the correct path description.

Let's copy SAMPLE2 from the NEWPARTS subdirectory to the OLDPARTS subdirectory using NCOPY.

1. You should still be in your home directory. Type

   CD NEWPARTS

   and then press the Enter key. You are changed to the NEW-PARTS subdirectory.

2. Substituting your volume and home directory name for SYS:HOME/JEFF, type

   NCOPY SAMPLE2 TO SYS:HOME/JEFF/OLDPARTS

   and then press the Enter key. The file is copied to OLDPARTS.

3. Change directories to OLDPARTS, type **DIR**, and then press the Enter key. The file SAMPLE2 appears in the directory list.

In Chapter 3, *Understanding DOS: The Disk Operating System*, you learned about the asterisk wildcard character (*), which allows you to copy more than one file from a directory. For example, typing *.DAT would copy all files with a .DAT extension, typing LETTER.* would copy all LETTER files, regardless of the extension, and *.* would copy *all* the files in the directory.

Until you are confident that you can specify accurate directory paths, always use DIR or NDIR to display a directory listing for the destination directory to make sure you copied the file correctly. If the file is not listed, look in the other directories along the path you entered. You may have left out part of the correct path, and thus copied the file to a directory short of the actual destination. Such slip-ups happen often, so don't panic if the file doesn't show up where you want it to.

Deleting Files

Imagine what your directories will look like after hundreds of files are created and moved about from directory to directory, or just sit there, having outlived their usefulness. You must be able to delete files that no longer serve any purpose in order to free up disk space for more important files. For example, when you copy a file from one directory to another, the original file remains in the first directory, and you end up with a copy of the file in both directories; the source file is usually redundant and should be deleted.

NetWare provides two ways of deleting files: the FILER menu utility and the DOS DEL command.

Using FILER to Delete Files

If you have completed the previous exercises in this chapter, you will have a copy of the file SAMPLE2 in your home directory, in the NEWPARTS subdirectory, and in the OLDPARTS subdirectory. Let's delete the copy of file SAMPLE2 that is in your home directory.

1. Change directories to your home directory.

2. At the DOS prompt, type **FILER** and press the Enter key. The Available Topics menu appears.

3. Move the highlight to File Information and press the Enter key. The current file list for your home directory is displayed.

4. Move the highlight to the file SAMPLE2 and press the Del key. The Delete File confirmation box appears (see Figure 7.12). If you want to delete more than one file, highlight each file and mark it by pressing the Mark key (F5). The Mark key selects one or more files to facilitate multifile deletions. (If F5 doesn't work for your keyboard, press F1 twice to see a list of function key assignments.) To unmark a marked file, highlight the file name and press the Mark key (F5) again. If the Delete File box does not appear, you do not have the security rights to delete files in that directory.

5. Move the highlight to Yes and press the Enter key. The file is deleted.

6. To exit FILER, press Esc twice.

7. At the Exit Filer box, press the Enter key. You are returned to the DOS prompt.

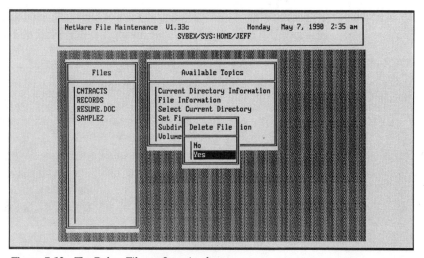

Figure 7.12: *The Delete File confirmation box*

Using the DEL Command to Delete Files

The DOS DEL command (Delete) works the same way on the network as it does on a DOS disk. You can delete a single file if you know the file name, or you can delete several files by using the wildcard *. Be careful when using the wildcard; you may delete valuable files that you wanted to keep. Refer to Chapter 3, *Understanding DOS: The Disk Operating System*, for more details about using the DEL command.

Let's use DEL to delete the file SAMPLE2 from the NEWPARTS subdirectory. You should currently be in your home directory.

1. To change directories to the NEWPARTS subdirectory, type **CD NEWPARTS** and press the Enter key.

2. At the DOS prompt, type **DEL SAMPLE2** and press the Enter key.

3. Type **DIR** and press the Enter key. The file SAMPLE2 is no longer listed.

Summary

In this chapter you learned how file attributes can be used to prevent access to files stored on the file server. The basic file security attributes are Read/Write, Read Only, Shareable, and Non-shareable. You also became familiar with some valuable file management tools, such as copying, renaming, and deleting files.

Understanding how to construct a path to identify the correct location of files that you want to work with is important if you want to manage your files effectively. If you're new to computers, it will take some time to become familiar with this concept, but with practice it won't take as long as you think. Remember, ask your supervisor for help whenever you get confused or lost; he or she will be more than glad to help you.

Chapter 8 introduces you to printing on the network.

Printing Your Documents

For most businesses, the expense of providing a printer for every computer, especially a costly laser printer, can be prohibitive. With a local area network (LAN), however, one printer can service every computer in the network.

NetWare provides a great deal of flexibility in the configuration of printers. A network setup can be as simple as one printer, that is attached to the file server and that handles *all* the print jobs. Or it can be as complex as five printers attached to each file server, plus additional printers located at the workstations. How your network printers are configured depends on the needs of the business and how much hardware the company can afford.

Printing on network printers is different from printing on a local printer. When you print a job locally, the document goes directly to the printer and is printed immediately. When you print on the network, the print job is sent to the file server, where it is placed in a print *queue*. NetWare uses print queues to organize the printing sequence of all print jobs sent to the file server. Each job is printed in the order in which it is received.

The network supervisor is responsible for setting up the printing environment for the network. How your network printing environment is set up depends on the needs of the business and the ingenuity of the network supervisor in meeting those needs. Some supervisors get very creative, designing elaborate combinations of network printers and print queues, while other supervisors use a printing setup that is established automatically when the network is installed. With this automatic setup, the NetWare operating system assigns one print queue to each printer attached to the file server, and every network user is assigned as a queue user for each printer.

These default print queues are assigned the names PRINTQ_0, PRINTQ_1, PRINTQ_2, and so on. The printers are correspondingly named Printer 0, Printer 1, Printer 2, and so on. The supervisor, as the queue operator, has the privilege of placing print jobs on hold, changing the position of a job in the queue, or deleting a job.

This chapter will introduce you to the basics of printing with NetWare. You'll learn how to send a print job to the file server with the NPRINT command. You'll also learn how to use the CAPTURE and ENDCAP commands to control whether your print jobs go to the network printer or your local printer.

Printing with NPRINT

The NetWare command line utility NPRINT is used to print DOS files or documents that have been printed to disk. (NPRINT will not print a document that is formatted in a data processing application.) Let's talk briefly about these two types of files.

Examples of DOS files are the README and MANUAL.DOC files that come with many software programs. These files contain valuable information about the software program and usually are written in ASCII (a standard format that can be used to send information between programs or computers), not the special computer language of a word processor like WordPerfect, for example. Using the NPRINT command line utility makes it possible to print out a hard copy of these important files.

You know about saving a file on a disk, but what does printing a file on a disk mean? If you create a document in an application, save it, and then try to print it with NPRINT, you'll only get garbage on the printout. But if you print the document to a disk file and print it with NPRINT, the document will print, preserving its formatted appearance. Therefore, if you want to send a copy of a document to another network user who doesn't have the same data processing application you have, you can print it to a disk file, and the other person can use NPRINT to print a copy of it. This situation arises often when users running different applications send files back and forth in networks with electronic mail. You can also save the document as an ASCII file and print it with NPRINT, but any special document formatting will be lost.

However, most of the time you will print your documents directly through your applications. Rarely will you need to use the NPRINT command. Remember, if you try to use NPRINT to print an application document, you will only get junk on the printed page.

Let's create a DOS text file using the COPY command and then print it on a network printer using NPRINT.

1. Turn your computer on and log in to the network.

2. Change to your home directory where you have all the rights to create, edit, save, and delete files.

3. At the DOS prompt, type

   COPY CON DOSPRINT

   and press the Enter key.

4. Type

   This is a DOS file printed with NPRINT.

   and press the Enter key.

5. Press Ctrl-Z and press the Enter key. This closes the DOS file.

Now that you have a file that will print with NPRINT, let's try it.

6. At the DOS prompt, type

   NPRINT DOSPRINT

   and press the Enter key. The DOS file DOSPRINT is sent to the file server print queue, where it waits its turn to print.

Printing with NPRINT is just that simple: type NPRINT and the file name at the DOS prompt, press the Enter key, and the file is shipped off to the file server.

If you want to get more creative with NPRINT, NetWare provides a number of options that you can use for specific job configurations. A job configuration specifies where and how you want the document to print. Table 8.1 lists the options you can select to set up your own job configuration.

Table 8.1: *The NPRINT Job Configuration Options*

To use one of these options, you may type the full command or just the letters shown in bold type. Unless specified, you may use more than one of these options in the same NPRINT command.

Option	Function
Server = *server*	Indicates which file server the data should be sent to, if other than your default server.

Table 8.1: *The NPRINT Job Configuration Options (cont.)*

Option	Function
Job = *job*	Specifies the name of a preset print job configuration. Supervisors and advanced users can set up print job configurations.
Printer = *n*	Indicates which printer attached to the file server will print the job. Replace *n* with the printer number. The default printer is P=O.
Queue = *queue*	Indicates which queue a print job is sent to. *Queue* is the print queue name.
Form = *form* or *n*	Indicates either the name or number of a form. Supervisors can define types of forms.
Copies = *n*	Indicates the number of copies to print. The limit is 256.
Tabs = *n*	Replaces tabs in your document with the number of spaces you specify (*n*). Used only when an application does not have a print formatter. You can specify up to 18 tab spaces.
NoTabs	Cancels all tab and control character interpretations by the queue print formatter (i.e., it prints the job "as is" with the special codes the application embedded in the document).
NAMe = *name*	Indicates the name that will go on the upper half of a banner. The default is your login username.
Banner = *banner*	Indicates the word to be displayed on the lower half of the banner. May be up to 12 characters with an underline character to represent spaces between words. The default banner word is the file name.
NoBanner	Used when you do not want to print a banner with your print job.
FormFeed	Sends a form feed when a print job has finished printing.

Table 8.1: *The NPRINT Job Configuration Options (cont.)*

Option	Function
NoFormFeed	Turns off end-of-job form feeds at the printer. Saves using a sheet of blank paper at the end of a print job.
CReate = *filename*	Sends data to a file, not to the printer. Include the directory path where the file is to be stored.
Delete	Automatically erases a file after you print it.

Your supervisor can establish for each user a default job configuration that NPRINT will use when printing. If such a job configuration has not been defined, NPRINT has its own defaults, which include these instructions:

- Send the print job to the default file server
- Place it in PRINTQ_0, which goes to Printer 0
- Print one copy
- Print a banner listing your username and the name of the file
- Issue a form feed at the end of the job
- Set ASCII tabs to eight spaces

To use a job configuration option with NPRINT, type the full name or the capitalized letter or letters of the option after the file name. Let's print DOSPRINT, the file you just created, using NPRINT and some of the more common options.

1. At the DOS prompt, type

   NPRINT DOSPRINT C = 2 NB

   and press the Enter key.

You just told NetWare to print two copies (C=2) of DOSPRINT without the banner (NB).

2. At the DOS prompt, type

   NPRINT DOSPRINT C = 1 B = HELLO

and press the Enter key.

You just told NetWare to print one copy (C=1) of the document with a banner (B=HELLO) that says HELLO. Your printed document should look like Figure 8.1.

Be sure and go to the network printer to pick up your print jobs. This exercise may be for practice, but if you send the job, it will print.

*P*rinting with the CAPTURE and ENDCAP Commands

Applications that are designed to work on a network can be set up to send print jobs directly to the file server. These networkable programs automatically differentiate between jobs destined for the network printer and those going to a local printer. However, a great many applications are not designed for networks. You can still run these applications on the network, but when you tell them to print, they send the job through one of your computer's parallel ports, which is used by a local printer.

The CAPTURE and ENDCAP commands provide you the means of controlling where your print jobs go. The CAPTURE command places an electronic net in front of the parallel port that "captures" the print job data and carries it to the file server for printing. As long as this net is in place, all print jobs directed through that port are captured and sent to the network. The ENDCAP (End Capture) command is used to turn the CAPTURE command off. When ENDCAP is used, the electronic net is removed and print jobs go to the local printer.

Using whatever application you have (a word processor works best for this exercise), let's use CAPTURE and ENDCAP in the following exercise. I am assuming you have a local printer connected to your PC. However, you can still do this exercise if you do not have a local printer.

1. If you aren't already logged in to the network, turn on your workstation and log in.

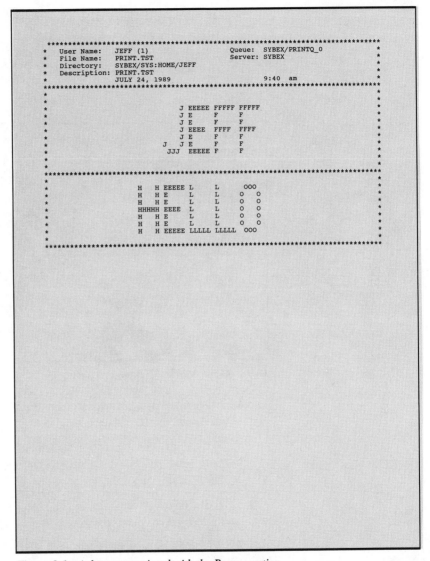

Figure 8.1: *A document printed with the Banner option*

2. Change to your home directory, where you should have all the rights to create, edit, save, and delete files.

3. Before you start your application, at the DOS prompt type

   CAPTURE

and press the Enter key. You will see a screen message similar to that in Figure 8.2. CAPTURE is on, the net is placed over parallel port 1, and print jobs sent to that port will go to the file server print queue.

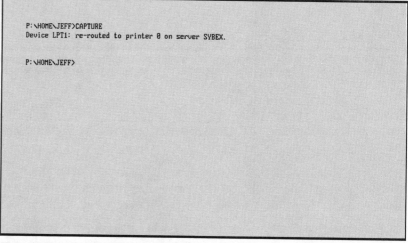

```
P:\HOME\JEFF>CAPTURE
Device LPT1: re-routed to printer 0 on server SYBEX.


P:\HOME\JEFF>
```

Figure 8.2: A CAPTURE screen message

4. Start your application and create a short document that you can send to the network printer.

5. When you complete the document, press the print keys for your application. Make sure the application is printing through LPT1. Otherwise, nothing will print.

6. Exit from your application. The print job is automatically sent to the file server print queue, where it waits in line to be printed.

7. At the DOS prompt, type

   ENDCAP

   and press the Enter key. You will see a screen message similar to the one in Figure 8.3. The capturing of LPT1 is now off and you can print on your local printer. If you do not have a local printer, you will have to use the CAPTURE command at this point to recapture LPT1 so you can print on the network printer.

```
P:\HOME\JEFF>ENDCAP
Device LPT1: set to local mode.


P:\HOME\JEFF>
```

Figure 8.3: An ENDCAP screen message

If you have an application that allows you to escape temporarily to a DOS prompt without shutting down the application, you can start the application *before* giving a CAPTURE command. Then create or edit your document and, when you're ready to print, escape to a DOS prompt and type **CAPTURE**. Return to your document, print it, escape back to DOS, and type **ENDCAP** so your next document will print at the local printer.

As with NPRINT, there are job configuration options you can use with CAPTURE and ENDCAP. See Table 8.2 for a list of these options.

Table 8.2: The CAPTURE and ENDCAP Job Configuration Options

To use one of these options, you may type the full command or just the letters shown in bold type. These options are used with CAPTURE.	
Option	**Function**
SHow	Displays current CAPTURE settings. Lists the file server, print queue, and printer port; lists the status of the banner, autoendcap, tabs, form feed, timeout, form, and copies to print. May not be used with any other CAPTURE option.

Table 8.2: *The CAPTURE and ENDCAP Job Configuration Options (cont.)*

Option	Function
Autoendcap	Sends data to the file server print queue when you exit an application. The LPT port remains captured for future print jobs.
NoAutoendcap	Prevents data from being sent to the file server print queue when you exit an application.
TImeout = n	The time (n), in seconds, between pressing an application's print keys and when the print job is sent to the file server. Replace n with any number from 1 to 1000. The default is 0.
Local = n	Indicates which LPT port is to be captured. Replace n with 1, 2, or 3. The default is LPT1. May also be entered as **LPT1**, **LPT2**, or **LPT3**.
Server = *server*	Indicates which file server the data should be sent to, if other than your default server.
Job = *job*	Specifies the name of a preset print job configuration. Supervisors and advanced users can set up print job configurations.
Printer = n	Indicates which printer attached to the file server will print the job. Replace n with the printer number. The default printer is P=0.
Queue = *queue*	Indicates which queue a print job is sent to. *Queue* is the print queue name.
Form = *form* or n	Indicates either the name or number of a form. Supervisors can define types of forms.
Copies = n	Indicates the number of copies to print. The limit is 256.
Tabs = n	Replaces tabs in your document with the number of spaces you specify (n). Used only when an application does not have a print formatter. You can specify up to 18 tab spaces.

Table 8.2: The CAPTURE and ENDCAP Job Configuration Options (cont.)

Option	Function
NoTabs	Cancels all tab and control character interpretations by the queue print formatter (i.e., it prints the job "as is," with special codes the application imbedded in the document). Used only if your application does not have a print formatter.
NAMe = *name*	Indicates the name that will go on the upper half of a banner. The default is your login username.
Banner = *banner*	Indicates the word to be displayed on the lower half of the banner. May be up to 12 characters with an underline character to represent spaces between words. The default banner word is *LST:*.
NoBanner	Used when you do not want to print a banner with your print job.
FormFeed	Sends a form feed when a print job has finished printing.
NoFormFeed	Turns off end-of-job form feeds at the printer. Saves using a sheet of blank paper at the end of a print job.
CReate = *filename*	Sends data to a file, not to the printer. Include the directory path where the file is to be stored.

These options are used with ENDCAP. You may use as many of these options in one ENDCAP command as you wish.

Local = *n*	Ends the capture of a specified LPT port. Replace the *n* with the number of the port—1, 2, or 3. May also be entered as **LPT1, LPT2,** or **LPT3.**
ALL	Ends the capture of all three LPT ports at once.
Cancel	Ends the capture of LPT1 and discards all data without printing it.
CancelLocal = *n*	Ends the capture of a specified LPT port and discards all data without printing it.
Cancel ALL	Ends the capture of all LPT ports and discards all data without printing it.

Always try to keep in mind the status of your printer ports when you print. The CAPTURE Show command, which you'll learn about next, will help you keep track of the port settings.

Chapters 9–11 include hands-on examples for using the CAPTURE and ENDCAP commands with WordPerfect, dBASE IV, and Lotus 1-2-3. Even if you do not use these applications, I recommend you read through the chapters just for the information on printing.

Using Options with the CAPTURE Command

The options that can be used with CAPTURE allow you to set up your own job configurations. When you send a document to the file server for printing, you can also send option commands that tell the operating system where and how to print the job. Let's experiment with a few of these options, using the Show option to see how a change of options affects a job configuration.

1. If you aren't already logged in to the network, turn on your workstation and log in.

2. At a DOS prompt, type

   CAPTURE SH

   and press the Enter key. You are presented with a display showing the current job configuration for the three parallel ports similar to the one in Figure 8.4. Refer to Table 8.2 for explanations of each item.

Let's change a few of the options.

3. At the DOS prompt, type

   CAPTURE C = 2 B = HAVING_FUN NAM = MIKE

   and press the Enter key.

4. At the DOS prompt, type **CAPTURE SH** and press the Enter key. Your screen display should show a changed job configuration for LPT1 similar to the one in Figure 8.5.

```
LPT1:   Capturing data to server SYBEX queue PRINTQ_0 (printer 0).
        Capture Defaults:Enabled      Automatic Endcap:Enabled
        Banner  :(None)               Form Feed       :No
        Copies  :1                    Tabs            :No conversion
        Form    :0                    Timeout Count   :3 seconds

LPT2:   Capturing Is Not Currently Active.

LPT3:   Capturing Is Not Currently Active.
```

Figure 8.4: *Job configuration for LPT1*

```
P:\HOME\JEFF>CAPTURE C=2 B=HAVING_FUN NAM=MIKE
Device LPT1: re-routed to printer 0 on server SYBEX.


P:\HOME\JEFF>CAPTURE SH

LPT1:   Capturing data to server SYBEX queue PRINTQ_0 (printer 0).
        Capture Defaults:Enabled      Automatic Endcap:Enabled
        Banner  :HAVING_FUN           Form Feed       :No
        Copies  :2                    Tabs            :No conversion
        Form    :0                    Timeout Count   :3 seconds

LPT2:   Capturing Is Not Currently Active.

LPT3:   Capturing Is Not Currently Active.
```

Figure 8.5: *A new job configuration for LPT1*

The job configuration now says you will print two copies of the document, with a banner with a username of MIKE that says HAVING FUN. If some of the other options have changed from the first time you viewed the options, don't worry about it; certain job configurations previously set up by your supervisor have caused the changes.

Let's try a few more options. Here you'll capture a port, send a form feed, and turn off the banner. (See Table 8.2 for an explanation of form feed.)

5. At the DOS prompt, type

   CAPTURE L = 2 FF NB

   and press the Enter key.

6. At the DOS prompt, type **CAPTURE SH** and press the Enter key. Figure 8.6 shows the new display. LPT1 AND LPT2 are both captured and list the options for each.

If you were to select LPT2 as the port to send the print job through, the document would print with form feed and no banner, as you just specified.

Now change the job configuration so that print jobs go through the file server.

7. At the DOS prompt, type

   ENDCAP ALL

   and press the Enter key. LPT1, LPT2, and LPT3 are no longer captured and are set to the local mode.

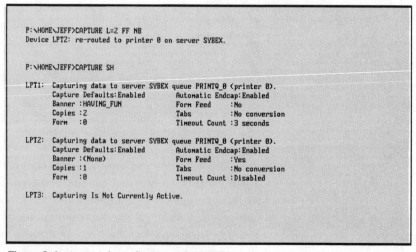

Figure 8.6: A new job configuration for LPT2

8. At the DOS prompt, type **CAPTURE SH** and press the Enter key. The display shows that capturing on all three parallel ports is not currently active (see Figure 8.7).

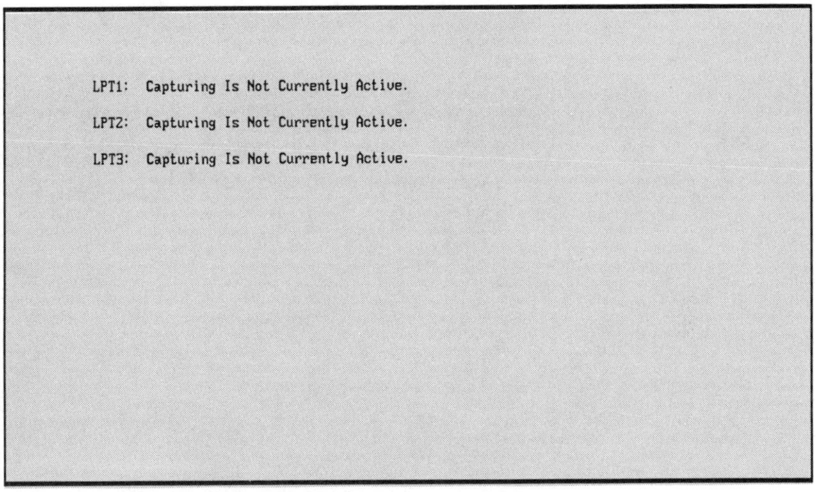

```
LPT1:  Capturing Is Not Currently Active.

LPT2:  Capturing Is Not Currently Active.

LPT3:  Capturing Is Not Currently Active.
```

Figure 8.7: LPT1, LPT2, and LPT3 not currently active

Summary

This chapter has been a brief but important discussion about network printing. NetWare is powerful and flexible, and is designed to anticipate your every printing need. You will most often be printing documents through your applications. Unless you have an application written for the network, you will have to use the CAPTURE and ENDCAP commands often. Your supervisor may even set up your login procedure to automatically capture your printer ports when you log in to the network. That way, you never have to use CAPTURE directly; you just print as you would on a stand-alone computer. Also, you may have LPT1 always in the local mode for using your local printer and have LPT2 captured to the network printer. All you do is select the proper printer from within your application, and the print job goes to the correct printer.

The setup variations are practically endless, but with what you've learned in this chapter, you will be able to send your print jobs to the correct printer. Remember, if you issue a print command and the document doesn't print where it's supposed to, don't keep trying to print it; see your supervisor immediately so he or she can help you find out where the print job went.

In Chapters 9–11, you will learn the basics of using WordPerfect, Lotus 1-2-3, and dBASE IV. If you are new to these programs and expect to use them on the network, I suggest you work through the exercises in each chapter. They will get you up and running quickly and easily.

NOVELL NETWARE

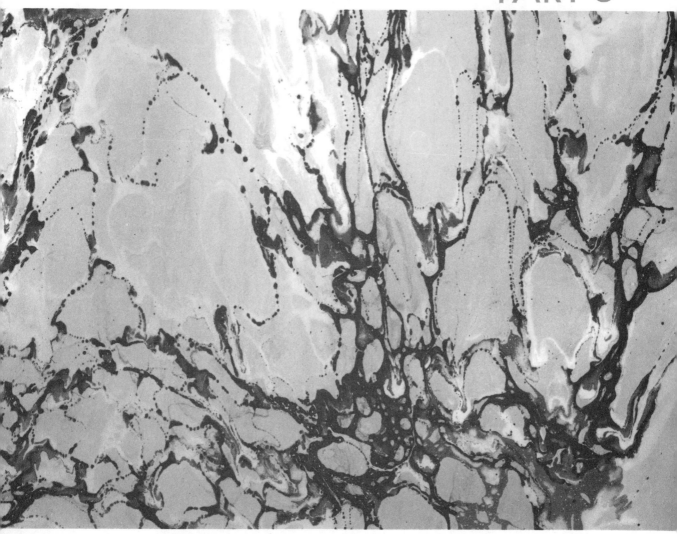

Using Applications with Novell NetWare

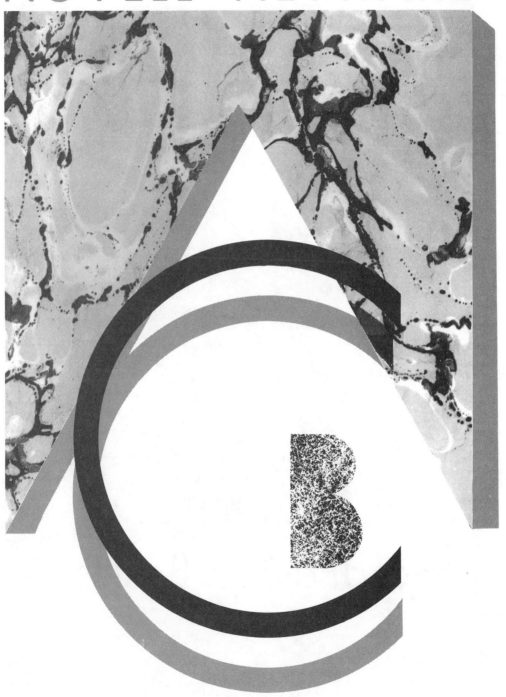

WordPerfect Basics

This chapter is primarily for those of you who are either new to Word-Perfect or are new to working on a network and need to get WordPerfect running so you can create that first document. I've spoken to secretaries who arrived at work one morning and discovered their typewriter had been replaced by a computer. Although they had never worked with a computer before, they were expected to produce documents that same day. "Panic" is too weak a word for their initial reaction. If you face, or may face, a similar challenge, the information in this chapter will show you how to start WordPerfect, create and edit a document, print it on the network, and save it for future editing.

Even if you have WordPerfect experience, I suggest you look briefly through this chapter. Some network procedures are mentioned that you might find beneficial, especially those that deal with printing on the network with WordPerfect.

WordPerfect is *the* word processor of choice for secretaries and business executives everywhere. It is one of the most popular word processing applications on the market, and once you get a little experience with it, you'll see why.

Working with WordPerfect on the Network

If you've used WordPerfect or any other word processor, you're used to running the program from the subdirectory where the program files are stored. On a network the procedure is different. The WordPerfect program files are stored on the file server, where they are shared by other network users. If every network user stored document files in the WordPerfect subdirectory on the file server, it would be difficult to figure out which file belonged to which user and extremely difficult to locate files.

How do you prevent problems like these? First of all, an efficiently organized directory structure is needed. In addition, a wise network supervisor will not allow users the trustee rights to edit, delete, or save files in the WordPerfect subdirectory. The supervisor will map a search drive to the subdirectory that contains the WordPerfect program files. You will be able to start WordPerfect from any subdirectory on the network, and the network operating system will look along the search-drive path, find the file that executes the WordPerfect program, and start the program. Then, when you save a document, it is stored directly in a subdirectory, where it can easily be found by those users who have the appropriate trustee rights. Use the MAP command (described in Chapter 6) to display a listing of your search-drive mappings. You should see a mapping to your WordPerfect subdirectory similar to the one in Figure 9.1. Notice the search-drive mappings to the Lotus 1-2-3 and dBASE IV subdirectories.

The chances of your not having a search drive mapped to your WordPerfect subdirectory are slim, but if you do not see one listed, ask your supervisor to create one for you.

```
SEARCH4:    = W:. [SYBEX/SYS:PROG/WP]
SEARCH5:    = V:. [SYBEX/SYS:PROG/123]
SEARCH6:    = U:. [SYBEX/SYS:PROG/DBASEIV]
```

Figure 9.1: *A search-drive mapping to the WordPerfect subdirectory*

Starting WordPerfect

With all this in mind, let's use the NEWPARTS subdirectory you created in Chapter 7 as your working directory for these exercises. If NEWPARTS no longer exists, use the MD command to create it (see Chapter 6 on how to create directories). Starting WordPerfect is an easy task.

1. Turn on your computer and log in to the network.

2. If you are at a DOS prompt, change to the NEWPARTS subdirectory. If you have a customized network menu, select the WordPerfect menu choice and press the Enter key.

3. If you have a DOS prompt, type **WP** and press the Enter key. You see the WordPerfect opening screen (Figure 9.2). If you have the network version of WordPerfect, you may see a prompt at the bottom of the screen asking you to enter a three-character username. Your initials are usually a good choice, although any three characters will do. Use this username every time you start WordPerfect. It is used to identify your setup file. This username is not related to your network username.

4. Type in the three characters and press the Enter key. The WordPerfect editing screen appears (see Figure 9.3).

WordPerfect presents you with a mostly blank screen, as though you were looking at a blank sheet of paper in a typewriter. The information in the lower-right corner of the screen tells you which document you are working on (with WordPerfect you can work on two documents at the same time), the page number, the line number indicating how far down the page the cursor is located, and the position of the cursor as it moves across the page when you enter text. The cursor always starts out in the upper-left corner. WordPerfect always starts you off in document 1, on page 1, and with top, bottom, left, and right margins of 1 inch.

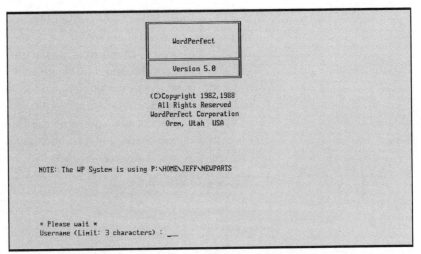

Figure 9.2: *WordPerfect opening screen and network username prompt*

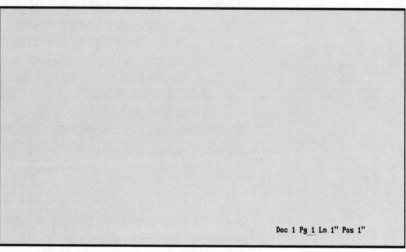

Doc 1 Pg 1 Ln 1" Pos 1"

Figure 9.3: *The WordPerfect editing screen*

Creating A WordPerfect Document

You can begin work immediately when you have the WordPerfect screen displayed on your monitor. For your first exercise, you will create a sample letter. With a few exceptions, the keyboard works much like a conventional typewriter. For example, you do not have to press the Enter (also called Return) key at the end of each line. Word-Perfect's word wrap feature automatically senses the right margin and wraps the sentence to the next line. You do, however, need to press the Enter key at the end of a paragraph.

Type the following text, pressing the Enter key as shown. Don't be concerned about correcting typing mistakes. I'll show you how to correct typos in a later section.

> **May 7, 1990 (Enter)**
> **(Enter)**
> **(Enter)**
> **(Enter)**
> **Ms. Bonnie Smith (Enter)**
> **1733 Oakwood Drive (Enter)**
> **Elwood, CA 92002 (Enter)**

(Enter)
(Enter)
(Enter)
Dear Ms. Smith: (Enter)
(Enter)
We received your request for tickets yesterday. Because of the immense interest in the Mendocino Shakespeare Festival, we have very few seats available for the dates you are interested in. We will do our best to accommodate you, however. (Enter)
(Enter)
Enclosed is a diagram of the theater seating. I've circled the seats I reserved for your requested dates. I will hold them for you unless I hear otherwise. (Enter)
(Enter)
Respectfully, (Enter)
(Enter)
(Enter)
(Enter)
Avery White (Enter)
Box Office Manager

Your letter should appear on your monitor screen as it does in Figure 9.4. Notice how the status line in the right corner of the screen has changed to reflect the new location of the cursor.

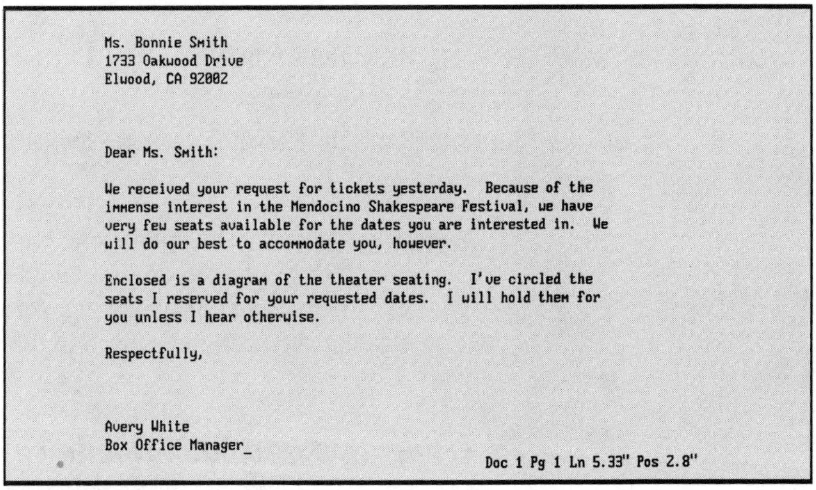

Ms. Bonnie Smith
1733 Oakwood Drive
Elwood, CA 92002

Dear Ms. Smith:

We received your request for tickets yesterday. Because of the immense interest in the Mendocino Shakespeare Festival, we have very few seats available for the dates you are interested in. We will do our best to accommodate you, however.

Enclosed is a diagram of the theater seating. I've circled the seats I reserved for your requested dates. I will hold them for you unless I hear otherwise.

Respectfully,

Avery White
Box Office Manager_

Doc 1 Pg 1 Ln 5.33" Pos 2.8"

Figure 9.4: *A sample letter*

Moving the Cursor

You saw in the previous exercise that the cursor indicates the position of each character that you type to the screen. If you want to edit your letter, you have to move the cursor to the desired location in the document. The four arrow keys you see on the right side of your keyboard (the Up Arrow key, the Down Arrow key, the Left Arrow key, and the Right Arrow key) are the *cursor movement keys*. These arrow keys are collocated with the numbered keys on the numeric keyboard. (On some keyboards, the arrow keys are separate from the numeric keyboard.) See Figure 9.5 for examples of different keyboard styles.

Press the Up Arrow key to move up the page, the Down Arrow key to move down, the Left Arrow key to move left, and the Right Arrow key to move right. If you press a key down and hold it, the cursor will move continuously in the direction of the arrow.

The cursor should be located at the end of your letter. Let's move the cursor to a new location in your document.

1. Press the Left Arrow key 18 times to move the cursor to the *B* in *Box Office Manager*.

2. Press the Up Arrow key nine times to move the cursor to the *E* in *Enclosed*.

3. Press the Right Arrow key 14 times to move the cursor to the *d* in *diagram*.

4. Press the Down Arrow key twice to move the cursor to the *e* in *hear*.

If you want to move the cursor one word at a time, press the Ctrl key and hold it down while you press the Left Arrow key or the Right Arrow key. Practice this on your own for a moment. When you are done, return the cursor to the letter *d* in the word *diagram*.

Inserting Text into Your Document

Editing a document often requires adding new text to the old. WordPerfect's Insert feature allows you to insert text anywhere you wish in a document. Let's add the word *photocopy* before the word *diagram*. The cursor should already be located on the *d* in *diagram*. If

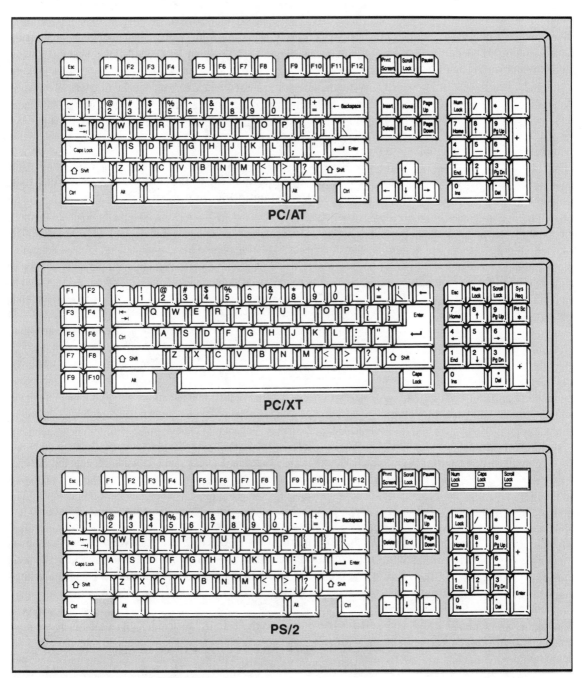

Figure 9.5: *The PC/AT, PC/XT, and PS/2 keyboards*

you see the word *Typeover* in the lower-left corner of your screen, press the Insert (Ins) key located on the right side of your keyboard to make it disappear. I'll explain Typeover in a moment.

1. With the cursor on the *d* in *diagram*, type the word *photo-copy*, pressing the space bar at the end of the word. You see *photocopy* inserted in front of *diagram*. The rest of the sentence is pushed to the right to make room.

2. Press the Down Arrow key and the sentence is wrapped to the next line, adjusting the text to the correct margins. Your text should look like that in Figure 9.6.

```
     Ms. Bonnie Smith
     1733 Oakwood Drive
     Elwood, CA 92002


     Dear Ms. Smith:

     We received your request for tickets yesterday.  Because of the
     immense interest in the Mendocino Shakespeare Festival, we have
     very few seats available for the dates you are interested in.  We
     will do our best to accommodate you, however.

     Enclosed is a photocopy diagram of the theater seating.  I've
     circled the seats I reserved for your requested dates.  I will hold
     them for you unless I hear otherwise.

     Respectfully,



     Avery White
     Box Office Manager_
                                            Doc 1 Pg 1 Ln 5.33" Pos 2.8"
```

Figure 9.6: *Inserted text*

Deleting Text

WordPerfect has many ways of deleting text, but we will only cover a couple of them in this introductory chapter. The Backspace key is used to delete one character at a time to the left of the cursor. The Delete key deletes the character at the cursor position. Let's try them both.

1. Move the cursor to the *o* in *of*, following the word *diagram*.

2. Press the Backspace key eight times to delete the word *diagram*. Again, press the Down Arrow key to adjust the text. Your new paragraph looks like the one in Figure 9.7.

3. Move the cursor to the *f* in *for*.

4. Press the Delete key eight times to delete the words *for you*. Notice the rest of the sentence is pulled forward as you delete each character located at the cursor position. Your edited document should look like the one in Figure 9.8.

```
Ms. Bonnie Smith
1733 Oakwood Drive
Elwood, CA 92002



Dear Ms. Smith:

We received your request for tickets yesterday.  Because of the
immense interest in the Mendocino Shakespeare Festival, we have
very few seats available for the dates you are interested in.  We
will do our best to accommodate you, however.

Enclosed is a photocopy of the theater seating.  I've circled the
seats I reserved for your requested dates.  I will hold them for
you unless I hear otherwise.

Respectfully,



Avery White
Box Office Manager_
                                            Doc 1 Pg 1 Ln 5.33" Pos 2.8"
```

Figure 9.7: *Deleting with the Backspace key*

```
Ms. Bonnie Smith
1733 Oakwood Drive
Elwood, CA 92002



Dear Ms. Smith:

We received your request for tickets yesterday.  Because of the
immense interest in the Mendocino Shakespeare Festival, we have
very few seats available for the dates you are interested in.  We
will do our best to accommodate you, however.

Enclosed is a photocopy of the theater seating.  I've circled the
seats I reserved for your requested dates.  I will hold them unless
I hear otherwise.

Respectfully,



Avery White
Box Office Manager_
                                            Doc 1 Pg 1 Ln 5.33" Pos 2.8"
```

Figure 9.8: *Deleting with the Delete key*

You now have enough information to go back through the entire letter and correct any typing errors you made earlier.

Using the Typeover Feature

I mentioned the Typeover feature earlier. With Typeover you can enter text on the top of existing text without pushing the rest of the sentence to the right. Be careful when using Typeover, however, because you can easily type over text you want to keep. Let's try it.

1. Move the cursor to the *o* in *otherwise* in the last sentence.

2. Press the Insert key. The Typeover prompt appears in the lower left corner of your screen. The Insert mode is now off.

3. Type the word *differently*, followed by a period. *Otherwise* is overwritten, not pushed to the right.

4. Press the Insert key to turn Typeover off and Insert on. The Typeover prompt disappears and Insert is turned on again. Your edited paragraph should look like the one in Figure 9.9.

Leave the letter document on the screen and move on to the next exercise.

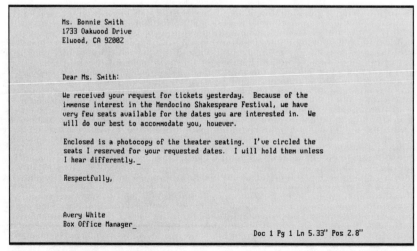

```
Ms. Bonnie Smith
1733 Oakwood Drive
Elwood, CA 92002


Dear Ms. Smith:

We received your request for tickets yesterday.  Because of the
immense interest in the Mendocino Shakespeare Festival, we have
very few seats available for the dates you are interested in.  We
will do our best to accommodate you, however.

Enclosed is a photocopy of the theater seating.  I've circled the
seats I reserved for your requested dates.  I will hold them unless
I hear differently._

Respectfully,



Avery White
Box Office Manager_
                                         Doc 1 Pg 1 Ln 5.33" Pos 2.8"
```

***Figure 9.9:** Editing with Typeover*

*P*rinting Your WordPerfect Document

The procedure you use to print a WordPerfect document depends on whether you have a networking or non-networking version of the program.

If you are using the networking version of WordPerfect 5, most of your printing procedures are simple. There is no need to use the CAPTURE and ENDCAP commands to direct your print jobs to the correct printer.

With a non-networking version, WordPerfect will send your print job directly to the network printer as long as your printer port is captured. (If you haven't read about capturing in Chapter 8, I suggest you do so before proceeding.)

Printing, especially on a network, can sometimes be a very frustrating experience, particularly when documents either don't print or print scrambled text. A network supervisor can set up a network for printing in a variety of ways, more than can be covered in this entry-level book. If you attempt to print and nothing happens, don't keep trying to print the document; contact your supervisor immediately so the problem can be corrected as soon as possible.

*P*rinting with the Network Version of WordPerfect

Your supervisor may have created a master setup file that selects all the printers the network users have access to, including both network and local printers. All you have to do is use WordPerfect to select the printer you want the job to print on, and WordPerfect does the rest.

In the following exercises, I used two printers: an HP LaserJet Series II laser printer attached to a file server, and a Standard Printer attached to a workstation. Your printers will probably be set up differently, but you can still do the exercises by selecting the printers you have available.

First, you'll use WordPerfect to select a printer. Then you'll print the sample letter you just created.

1. Press the Print key (Shift-F7) by pressing the Shift key and holding it down while pressing the F7 key. WordPerfect presents

you with the menu shown in Figure 9.10. In the Options part of the menu, you see an HP LaserJet Series II printer currently selected. Your selected printer may be different.

2. To select a printer different from the one listed, choose the Select Printer option by pressing the S key. The Select Printer menu appears (see Figure 9.11).

Your menu may offer more or fewer printers than are shown in Figure 9.11, but you'll always have one listed, or you can't print. In this example, the Standard Printer is the local printer connected to the workstation. Remember, you must select the correct printer type and model, regardless of the location. If you select the wrong printer driver, the printer will not be able to understand the codes sent by the program, causing it to print junk. The location of the printer, whether it is local or on the server, was determined when you or the supervisor edited the printer configuration. To view the configuration and determine where the output is being directed, press E or 3 for the printer that is reverse highlighted in the printer selection screen. Do not change any settings without consulting your supervisor.

3. From the Select Printer menu, select a printer you want to print on. Place the highlight on the correct printer and press 1

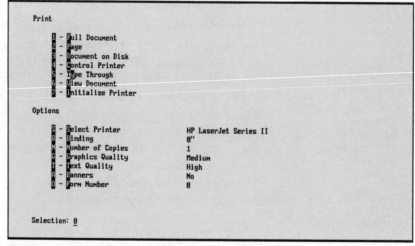

Figure 9.10: The WordPerfect Print menu (network version)

or S. You are returned to the Print menu. If you chose a different printer, you will see it listed on the menu (see Figure 9.12).

4. Press 1 or F to print the entire document or 2 or P to print the page the cursor is located on. You are returned to your document screen.

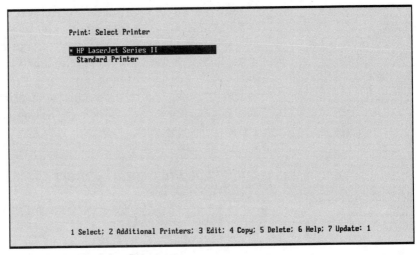

Figure 9.11: *The Select Printer menu*

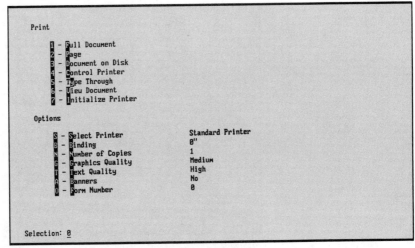

Figure 9.12: *The newly selected printer is listed*

Your print job is sent to the file server print queue, where it will wait its turn to be printed.

*P*rinting with a Non-Network Version of WordPerfect

Usually, the network supervisor will set up the system login script to automatically capture the printer port on your workstation when you log in, thereby ensuring that print jobs go to the file server queue and subsequently print on the network printers. You do not have to manually enter the CAPTURE command unless you want to send the print job through a different port.

The following exercises assume your printer port is captured to the network file server. Let's look at printing both to the network printer and your local printer.

Printing on the Network Printer

1. The WordPerfect Print key is Shift-F7. Press the Shift key and hold it down while pressing the F7 key. WordPerfect presents you with the Print menu shown in Figure 9.13.

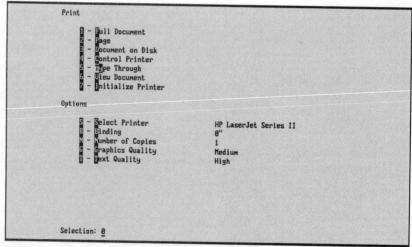

Figure 9.13: The WordPerfect Print menu (non-network version)

2. Press 1 or F to print the entire document or 2 or P to print one page. Either of these keys will print your one-page letter. You are returned to your document screen, and the print job goes to the file server print queue, where it waits its turn to be printed.

If the letter prints on your local printer instead of the network printer, your printer port is not captured. Follow these steps to capture the print job to the file server.

1. Press the Shell key, Ctrl-F1. You will see a prompt in the lower-left corner of your screen that looks like this:

   1 Go to DOS: 0

2. Press 1 or G and you will temporarily exit out of WordPerfect to a DOS prompt. WordPerfect is still running.

3. At the DOS prompt, type **CAPTURE** and press the Enter key. You will receive a message saying your printer port has been routed to the file server print queue.

4. At the DOS prompt, type **EXIT** and press the Enter key. You are returned to WordPerfect.

5. Press Shift-F7 and select 1 or F to print the entire document or 2 or P to print the page the cursor is located on. Your print job is sent to the file server.

Printing on Your Local Printer

If you want to print at a local printer connected to your workstation, you will have to turn the CAPTURE command off with the ENDCAP command. If you forget to use ENDCAP, you might try to print the document several times in a vain effort to make something happen at your local printer. If you keep trying, an unhappy supervisor might show up at your workstation lugging several copies of your 30-page document, all of which have been printed on the network printer. It won't be a pretty sight.

Again, let's assume your workstation is set up to send print jobs to the file server, but you want to print on your local printer. If the local printer is different than the one you were using on the network, you must change the printer type before printing (Shift-F7,S).

1. Press the Shell key, Ctrl-F1. You will see a prompt in the lower-left corner of your screen:

   1 Go to DOS: 0

2. Press 1 or G. You temporarily exit WordPerfect to a DOS prompt. WordPerfect is still running.

3. At the DOS prompt, type **ENDCAP** and press the Enter key. You will receive a message saying your printer port is set to the local printer.

4. At the DOS prompt, type **EXIT** and press the Enter key. You return to your document in WordPerfect.

5. Press Shift-F7 and select 1 or F, then 2 or P. Your document prints at your local printer.

To return to printing on the network printer, exit to DOS again (Ctrl-F1, 1 or G), and type **CAPTURE**, plus any options you want, at the DOS prompt. You will again have your print jobs captured at the printer port and sent to the file server.

Saving a Document

Once you create your documents you will want to save them onto the file server hard disk so you can retrieve them later for editing. You can save the document either while you are still working on it or when you are finished with it and are ready to exit WordPerfect.

Saving without Exiting

I recommend you save your document every 10 or 15 minutes in case there is a power failure and your workstation or the file server goes down. If you leave your workstation for any reason while preparing a document, make it a habit to save your work first. It's an easy process.

Let's save this letter under the file name TICKETS.LTR.

1. Press F10, the Save key. You will see this prompt in the lower-left corner of your screen:

   Document to be Saved:

2. Type

   TICKETS.LTR

   and press the Enter key. The letter is saved in the NEWPARTS subdirectory. If you want to save the document to another subdirectory, you must type in the complete path name.

Saving and Exiting WordPerfect

When you are finished with your word processing chores, you will want to save your latest document and exit WordPerfect. It is important that you always exit the program with the Exit key (F7). Exiting improperly causes WordPerfect to think the program is still running the next time you start up. If this ever happens, you will see the following prompt on the WordPerfect opening screen:

Are other copies of WordPerfect currently running? (Y/N)

Simply press N to start WordPerfect. Let's save TICKETS.LTR once more and then exit the program.

1. Press F7, the Exit key. You will see this prompt in the lower-left corner of your screen:

   Save document? (Y/N) Yes

2. Press Y or the Enter key. You will see a prompt followed by the current name of the file plus the directory path name. For example

   Document to be saved:
   P:\HOME\JEFF\NEWPARTS\TICKETS.LTR

   You may change the path to another subdirectory and/or the file name by typing in the new information.

3. Press the Enter key to accept the currently displayed name. You will see the following prompt:

   Replace *current file name*? (Y/N)

   This prompt alerts you that the old version of this newly edited file will be overwritten. Usually, you no longer need the old version, so you want to go ahead and replace it.

4. Press Y. The file is saved and you see this prompt:

   Exit WP? (Y/N) N

5. Press Y to exit to a DOS prompt.

*S*ummary

You have learned how to start WordPerfect, how to create, edit, and save documents, and how to print them on the network printer or your local printer using the CAPTURE and ENDCAP commands. This chapter barely scratches the surface of what WordPerfect can do. For example, WordPerfect also has powerful desktop publishing features for incorporating graphics into your documents. For those who require a more thorough presentation of the many features offered by WordPerfect, SYBEX publishes several books on WordPerfect, ranging from beginning to advanced levels.

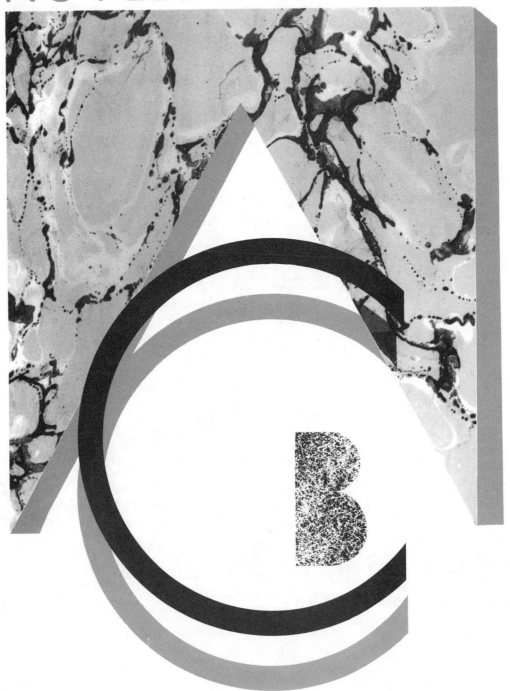

NOVELL NETWARE

Lotus 1-2-3 Basics

If budgets, invoices, annual reports, loan analyses, and tax statements are part of your job, then Lotus 1-2-3 is the program for you. If you have no experience with 1-2-3 or are new to working on a network, this chapter is designed to get you up and running as quickly as possible. Even if you are experienced with 1-2-3 on a stand-alone computer, however, I recommend that you quickly read through these exercises to see how the program operations may be affected when working on the network. The network printing procedures are especially important.

Because this is an entry-level book, this chapter is limited to the basics of 1-2-3. You will learn how to start 1-2-3 on the network, interpret the worksheet and place data in it, edit the data, print it, and save it for future editing. Additional powerful features in 1-2-3 not covered here include a graphics program and a database management program.

*W*orking with 1-2-3 on the Network

The Lotus 1-2-3 program is stored in its own subdirectory on the network file server. The spreadsheet data files will normally be stored in a subdirectory separate from the 1-2-3 program files, making it easier to locate data files for editing.

Usually, each user of 1-2-3 will have a network drive mapped to the subdirectory in which they will save their files. If working with spreadsheets is your only job, you will probably be automatically transferred to that subdirectory when you log in.

The network supervisor will also map a search drive to the 1-2-3 program subdirectory, enabling you to start the program from any subdirectory on the network. Use the MAP command to display a list of all your drive mappings (see Chapter 6). You should see a search-drive mapping to your 1-2-3 program subdirectory similar to the one in Figure 10.1. If you do not have this search-drive mapping, ask your supervisor to create one for you.

Each network has its own specific directory organization based on the number of workstations and the job requirements. Variations on this structure are endless, so I suggest you ask your supervisor to provide you with a diagram of the directory structure, including the subdirectories that have been set up for you.

```
SEARCH4:  = W:. [SYBEX/SYS:PROG/WP]
SEARCH5:  = V:. [SYBEX/SYS:PROG/123]
SEARCH6:  = U:. [SYBEX/SYS:PROG/DBASEIV]
```

Figure 10.1: A search-drive mapping to the 1-2-3 subdirectory

Starting 1-2-3

Unless it is company procedure, I recommend never starting 1-2-3 from the 1-2-3 program subdirectory. It's too easy to forget and save your worksheets directly in that subdirectory, instead of saving them in the document subdirectory.

If your network has a customized menu (see the example shown in Figure 10.2) you may be able to activate the 1-2-3 program from a menu selection.

I will assume you have a search drive mapped to the program files for 1-2-3. For the purposes of these exercises, let's create a sample worksheet in the OLDPARTS subdirectory you created in your home directory in Chapter 7. If OLDPARTS no longer exists, use the MD command to create it (see Chapter 6).

1. Turn on your computer and log in to the network. If you log in to the network to a customized menu, you will probably be able to select 1-2-3 on the menu to start the program. For the purposes of this exercise, however, you'll start 1-2-3 from a DOS prompt.

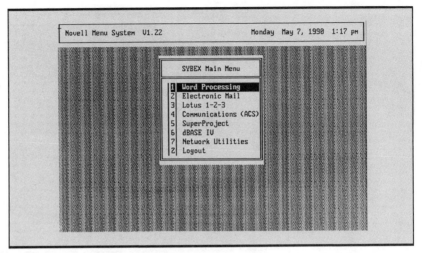

Figure 10.2: *A customized NetWare menu*

2. Change directories to the OLDPARTS subdirectory. If you have a customized menu, you can escape to a DOS prompt to do this.

3. At the DOS prompt, type

   123

   and press Enter. The 1-2-3 worksheet appears on your monitor screen (see Figure 10.3).

Figure 10.3 has labels describing the key work areas on the worksheet. These items are explained in more detail in the following section.

*T**he 1-2-3 Worksheet*

The 1-2-3 worksheet is where you create your spreadsheet documents. What you see on your screen is actually the upper-left corner of a very large worksheet. The worksheet has several key work areas (see the labels in Figure 10.3) that you'll need to become familiar with before creating your first document.

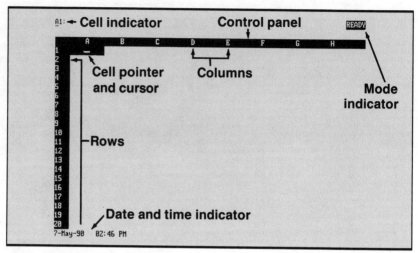

Figure 10.3: *The 1-2-3 worksheet*

Columns are designated by capital letters A-Z that run across the top of your spreadsheet. When you reach Z, the next column heads are labeled AA, AB, AC, and so on. When you reach AZ, they become BA, BB, BC, until you reach IV, which is column 256. Of the total of 256 columns, only 8 are visible at any one time. The rest of them disappear off the right side of the screen.

Rows are designated by numbers that run down the left edge of the worksheet and disappear off the bottom of the screen. You can have as many as 8,192 rows in a spreadsheet.

A *cell* is an area on the spreadsheet where a column and a row intersect. The *cell indicator* displays the column (A) and the row (1) where the *cell pointer and cursor* is located; this is the current, or active cell. The current cell is always highlighted. A cell is initially nine characters wide.

The cell pointer points to the location where data is entered into the worksheet. The *cursor* is the small flashing line inside the cell pointer. It moves between the work area and the control panel and indicates where keyboard characters are typed.

The control panel displays the command inputs, menus, prompts, and formulas used to create the worksheet. It is blank until you enter commands or make a menu request.

The mode indicator indicates the current status of the job in progress during construction of a worksheet. It currently says READY, indicating the worksheet is waiting for input.

The date and time indicator indicates the date and time your worksheet was created.

*M*oving the Cell Pointer

Before you begin work on your spreadsheet, take a few moments to learn how to move the cell pointer. I mentioned earlier that the cell pointer points to the cell where data is entered in the worksheet. When you start 1-2-3, the cell pointer is in cell A1. Let's use the cursor arrow keys to move the pointer to several different cells. When you use arrow keys that are collocated with the numeric keypad, make sure the Num Lock key is toggled off, otherwise 1-2-3 will think you are entering numerical data into the worksheet.

1. Press the Right Arrow key five times. The pointer moves to cell F1. Notice the cell indicator in the upper-left corner changes to F1.

2. Press the Down Arrow key five times. The pointer moves to cell F6.

3. Press the Left Arrow key three times. The pointer moves to cell C6.

4. Press the Home key. The pointer moves back to cell A1. The Home key brings the pointer back to A1 from any location on the worksheet.

5. Press the Page Down key. The pointer moves down one full screen, or 20 rows. You are now at cell A21.

6. Press the Page Up key. The pointer moves up one full screen, or 20 rows. The pointer returns to cell A1.

Now try this handy method to move quickly to a predetermined location on the worksheet.

7. Press the F5 function key and look at the control panel. You see the prompt

   Enter address to go to: A1

   Type **G12** and press Enter. The pointer moves to cell G12.

8. Press the Home key to move the pointer back to cell A1 for the next exercise.

Holding a cursor key down will cause the pointer to move continuously. When the cursor runs into the edge of the worksheet, you will hear a beep that alerts you to release the cursor key.

Constructing a 1-2-3 Worksheet

In this section I will take you through each step in constructing a Lotus spreadsheet. You'll learn how to enter labels and values, perform calculations, and use 1-2-3 commands to save and print your worksheet and exit the program. These basic operations will get you started, and in no time at all you'll be ready to use the more sophisticated features of 1-2-3.

Labeling the Worksheet

The columns and rows of numbers that make up a spreadsheet will have no meaning unless you label them. You can have many different kinds of labels: years, months, days, dates, quarters, subject titles—you name it, you can have a label for it. For these exercises we'll use labels for a simple monthly profit and loss statement.

If you make an error typing a label, use the Backspace key to correct it *before* you press an arrow key to move the pointer to the next cell. Don't try to place the pointer back on the cell to correct a mistake after you've moved the pointer. In a moment you'll learn how to correct an entry that is already placed in the cell.

1. Begin by typing the label for the title of the worksheet. With the pointer in cell A1, type

   MAY 1990; USED PARTS PROFIT/LOSS FIGURES

Do not press the Enter key. Your worksheet will look like Figure 10.4. Notice the mode indicator in the upper-right corner of the screen changes from READY to LABEL. The label is typed into the control panel so it may be edited before it is placed in the worksheet. If you used the Caps Lock key to type the label, the CAPS indicator appears in the lower-right corner of the screen.

2. Press the Down Arrow key twice and the Right Arrow key once to move the pointer to cell B3. The label is placed in the worksheet at cell A1.

Now you're ready to type the labels for the columns and position them within the cell. The following prefixes provided by 1-2-3 allow you to position a label within a cell. These prefixes are simply typed in before the text of the label.

Prefix	Label Location
^	Centers the label in the cell
'	Aligns the label with the left edge of the cell
"	Aligns the label with the right edge of the cell
\	Repeats the label across the width of the cell

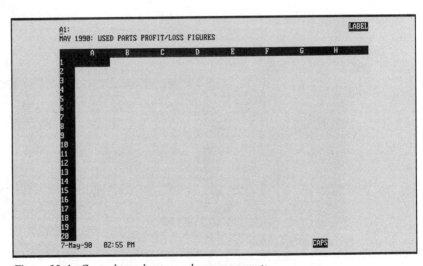

Figure 10.4: *Control panel entry and screen prompts*

Let's center the label in the cell.

3. Type ^**Week 1** and press the Right Arrow key. The pointer moves to cell C3. The caret (^) symbol places the label in the center of the nine-space cell.

4. In cell C3, type ^**Week 2**. Press the Right Arrow key to move to cell D3 and type ^**Week 3**. Press the Right Arrow key to move to cell E3 and type ^**Week 4**, then press the Right Arrow key again.

You now have a row of labels, each of which is centered in its respective cell. Complete the column labels by placing a double-dashed line under the weekly column headings.

5. Press F5 and type **B4** and then press the Enter key. The pointer moves to cell B4.

6. Type \= and press the Right Arrow key. The Backslash key (\) tells 1-2-3 to repeat the equal sign label across the nine cell spaces.

7. Repeat step 6 for cells B4 through E4 to place the = symbols under all the Week labels. Your worksheet should now look like Figure 10.5.

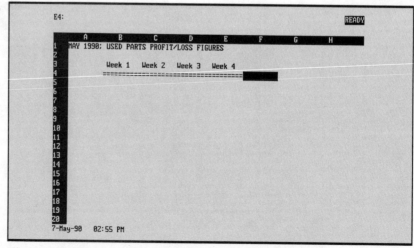

Figure 10.5: *The worksheet with the title and column labels*

Now add the labels for the rows. You'll type ten labels for the income and expense data.

8. Press F5 and type **A5** and then press the Enter key. The pointer moves to cell A5.

9. In cell A5, type

    ^INCOME

    and press the Down Arrow key.

The next label begins with a number. If the label begins with a number, you must always use the apostrophe (') in front of the number. 1-2-3 interprets numbers as numerical values entered on the worksheet for calculation purposes. If you forget the apostrophe, 1-2-3 will beep at you because it won't accept numerical entries with letters in them.

10. In cell A6, type

    '1- Auto

    and press the Down Arrow key. The apostrophe tells 1-2-3 that the number 1 is part of a label, not a value to be entered for calculation purposes. It also causes the label to be lined up with the left edge of the cell.

11. In cell A7, type

    '2- Body

    and press the Down Arrow key.

12. In cell A8, type

    TTL INC

    and press the Down Arrow key twice.

13. In cell A10, type

    ^EXPENSES

    and press the Down Arrow key.

14. In cell A11, type

    '1- Rent

and press the Down Arrow key.

15. In cell A12, type

    '2- Parts

and press the Down Arrow key.

16. In cell A13, type

    '3- Taxes

and press the Down Arrow key.

17. In cell A14, type

    TTL EXP

and press the Down Arrow key twice.

18. In cell A16, type

    PRFT/LOSS

and press the Enter key. Your worksheet should look like the one in Figure 10.6.

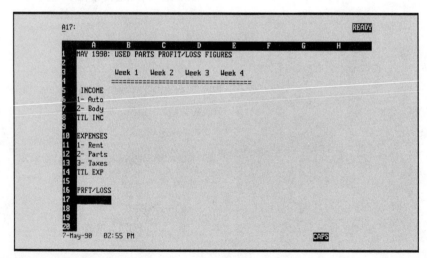

Figure 10.6: *Worksheet labels*

The labels across the page divide the month into four weeks, and the labels down the left edge of the worksheet are the items to be calculated. The next step is to place values for each item in the correct cell.

Placing Values in Cells

Values are the numerical input for each item that you want 1-2-3 to do calculations on. In this exercise, you'll place numbers that represent dollars in the Week 1 column. When you type in a value, you'll see it entered on the control panel before it gets placed in the worksheet. If you make a mistake, use the Backspace key to correct it before you press the Enter key or the arrow key that places the number in its cell. Do not place a label prefix before a value.

1. Press the F5 key, type **B6**, and press Enter. The pointer moves to cell B6, the intersection of Week 1 and 1- Auto.

2. Type **2000** and press the Down Arrow key. The pointer moves to cell B7.

3. Type **1000** and press the Down Arrow key four times. The pointer moves to cell B11.

4. Type **500** and press the Down Arrow key. The pointer moves to cell B12.

5. Type **1200** and press the Down Arrow key. The pointer moves to cell B13.

6. Type **1000** and press the Enter key. All the values for Week 1 are entered. Your worksheet should look like the one in Figure 10.7.

Before you learn about applying formulas to calculate the total income, total expenses, and profit and loss figures, let's take a look at correcting errors that slip by at the time of entry.

Correcting Mistakes with the F2 Key

Correcting label or numerical entries is not as simple as placing the pointer back on the entry and changing the value. You must make

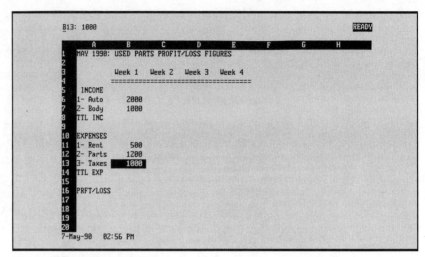

Figure 10.7: *Worksheet values*

your changes at the control panel. The F2 function key allows you to pick up a label or value, place it back in the control panel, edit it, and then return it to the correct cell. It's very easy.

1. The pointer should still be in cell B13. Press F5, the Go To key, then type **B6** and press the Enter key. The pointer moves to cell B6.

2. Press the F2 key. The value is automatically placed into the control panel at the top of the screen.

3. Move the highlight to the 2 in 2000 and press the Delete key. The number 2 is deleted.

4. Type **3** and press the Enter key. The corrected value is placed back in cell B6.

*U*sing Formulas and Functions

Thus far you've used labels to build the "container" that holds your income and expense figures, and you've poured the figures into the container. Now it's time to shake up the container and see how the numbers come together. This is when the magic takes place.

Formulas can be as simple or as complex as necessary to get the job done. Once you determine what mathematical processes you need, you can standardize your procedures and use these same formulas over and over again. This chapter only scratches the surface of the mathematical functions available to you. Your Lotus 1-2-3 documentation provides a complete list of functions.

You tell 1-2-3 to perform a mathematical function by typing a symbol called an *operator*. Here is a list of some of the most commonly used mathematical operators:

Operator	Function
+	Addition (or to indicate a positive number)
−	Subtraction (or to indicate a negative number)
*	Multiplication
/	Division. (Think of the / symbol as the divisor line in a fraction such as 3/4, which means 3 divided by 4.)
^	Exponentiation

When entering worksheet values into a formula, it is not necessary to enter the number. Instead, you can enter the cell identifier. For example, to obtain the total income from Auto and Body on your sample worksheet, you would enter the formula +B6+B7, or 3000+1000. The plus sign in front of B6 is necessary to prevent 1-2-3 from thinking the formula is a label. If you forget the plus sign, the formula will be written in a cell on the worksheet and will not perform the calculation you intended it to perform.

Sometimes formulas can become long and cumbersome. Let's look at the sample worksheet you just created. To compute the overall profit and loss for Week 1, you total your income first, then the expenses, and finally subtract the expenses from the income. The formula would look like this:

+ B6 + B7 − (B11 + B12 + B13)

This translates to

Auto + Body − (Rent + Parts + Taxes)

The parentheses tell 1-2-3 to add the enclosed items first and then subtract that sum from the first part of the equation. Using parentheses is essential if you are to obtain accurate results in formulas that combine multiplication and division with addition and subtraction, as well as in other more complex calculations.

For example, the formula $6-3*2$ could be calculated in two different ways. If you first subtract 3 from 6, you're left with 3. If you then multiply this 3 by the 2, the final result is 6. On the other hand, if you multiply 3 times 2 first, the answer is 6. If you then subtract this 6 from 6, the answer is 0. So, if you want to subtract first, you write the equation like this: $(6-3)*2$. Because of the parentheses, 1-2-3 knows to subtract first and then multiply.

The @SUM function is invaluable when you are working with long formulas. This function lets you shorten a line of entries into a more manageable package. The following sample worksheet formula (which you saw above)

> + B6 + B7 − (B11 + B12 + B13)

could be written

> + B6 + B7 − @SUM(B11 . . B13)

The formula reads, "Add B6 and B7 and then subtract the sum of B11 through B13."

Admittedly, in this example the @SUM function hardly shortens the formula, but you can nevertheless see that when you have a very long spreadsheet with many numbers in the columns, the @SUM function could become very useful. Instead of typing every cell identifier in the column, you type only the first and last cell identifiers with two dots in between.

Let's use formulas on your sample worksheet to determine your Week 1 profit and loss. You may use uppercase or lowercase letters when typing in formulas. Do not type any spaces into the formulas.

1. Move the pointer to cell B8. This is the cell that will contain the total of your Week 1 income.

2. Type **+B6+B7**. Before you press the Enter key, check to see you've entered the formula correctly. The mode indicator in the upper-right corner changes to VALUE.

3. Press the Enter key. The calculated value of 4000 appears in cell B8. 1-2-3 remembers this formula, and if you ever change the value in cells B6 or B7, the value in cell B8 will automatically be recalculated.

Now use the @SUM function to add the expenses.

4. Move the pointer to cell B14 and type

   @SUM

You now have two choices. You can type *B11..B13)*, or you can use the pointer to select the cells you want to use in the formula. Let's use the pointer to complete the formula.

5. Move the pointer to cell B11 and type a period. The B11 value is entered in the formula, followed by two periods and B11 again.

6. Move the pointer to cell B13, highlighting cells B11 through B13. The second B11 in the equation is replaced by cell B13.

7. Type a closed parenthesis to finish the formula and press the Down Arrow key. The total value of the sum of cells B11 through B13 is seen in cell B14: 2700.

Now calculate the profit/loss value in cell B16 by pointing.

8. Move the pointer to cell B16 and type a plus sign.

9. Move the pointer to cell B8 (total income) and press the minus sign. The pointer jumps back to B16 and you see +B8− in the control panel.

10. Move the pointer to cell B14 (total expenses) and press the Enter key. The pointer again jumps back to cell B16 and enters the total profit/loss calculation: 1300. The formula appears in the control panel.

Figure 10.8 below shows you the completed worksheet.

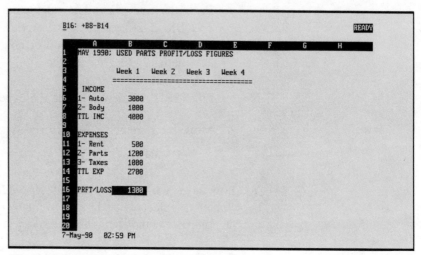

Figure 10.8: USED PARTS PROFIT/LOSS results

Editing a Spreadsheet

Being able to replace any value and having the entire worksheet recalculate itself is an incredible bit of magic not to be taken for granted. If you've had to spend countless hours rerecording entries and recalculating totals on a ledger sheet, then you will appreciate the power of 1-2-3 the first time you edit a worksheet.

Playing the "What if" Game

What if the profit and loss statement you just created was a *forecasted* profit and loss statement? And what if your landlord says he's going to raise your rent from $500 per week to $650 per week in May of 1990? How is this rent increase going to affect your profit and loss forecast? It's easy to figure this out if you let 1-2-3 do it for you. Let's see how it works.

1. Move the pointer to cell B11 (rent) and type **650**.

2. Press Enter. The TTL EXP cell, B14, is immediately recalculated along with the PRFT/LOSS cell, B16 (see Figure 10.9).

The Command Line Menu

The command line menu contains the procedures used to manipulate a worksheet during and after its creation. To see the command line, press the slash key (/, the same key with the question mark). A menu of 1-2-3 commands appears on the control panel (see Figure 10.10).

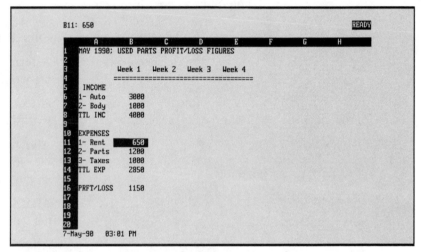

Figure 10.9: *The worksheet with new calculations*

Figure 10.10: *The command line menu*

The first line displays the ten major categories of commands. The second line displays minor commands that are associated with each major category. When you select a new major command, this second line automatically presents a new set of minor commands. The Worksheet command is initially highlighted, and the mode indicator changes to MENU.

Although we will not investigate each of these commands in detail, I would like to introduce you to each major category.

Command Category	Function
Worksheet	Affects the entire appearance of the worksheet.
Range	Affects only a portion of the worksheet.
Copy	Allows you to move a section of the worksheet to another location on the worksheet.
Move	Allows you to move data within the worksheet.
File	Allows you to retrieve, save, and erase files.
Print	Allows you to print a worksheet.
Graph	Allows you to turn a worksheet into a graphic representation.
Data	Provides the means to develop a database.
System	Allows you to temporarily exit 1-2-3. You can then execute DOS commands or run other programs, then return to your worksheet. You can also format new floppy disks through DOS.
Quit	Used to exit 1-2-3 when your work is done.

Saving the Worksheet

After you've created the worksheet, you'll want to save it for future editing. It's a good idea to occasionally save your worksheet while you're creating it. If the power cord accidentally gets pulled or there's a power failure, you'll lose all your work if it's not saved onto a disk.

When you save your worksheet, you will be asked to give it a file name. There are three rules to remember when assigning a file name to a worksheet:

- Limit the name to eight characters. 1-2-3 automatically assigns the file extension .WK1 to each file. (In versions of 1-2-3 prior to 2.0, files are saved with a .WK? extension.)

- Use only letters, numbers, and the underline key when naming files.

- Do not use punctuation marks or spaces in a file name.

You use the File command when you save your worksheets. Let's save your newly created worksheet in the OLDPARTS subdirectory under the name of PLMAY90.

1. Press the slash key (/) to display the command line menu. The highlight is on Worksheet.

2. Move the highlight to the File command with the Right Arrow key. The second command line changes to the minor commands associated with the File category (see Figure 10.11).

3. Press the Enter key. The minor commands are available for selection.

4. Move the highlight to the Save command and press the Enter key. You see a prompt similar to the following:

Enter save file name: P:\HOME\JEFF\OLDPARTS*.WK1

1-2-3 automatically enters the current directory path where the file will be stored. You will also see a list of worksheet files for that directory that have been saved in the past.

The procedures for saving new files and files that have been saved before are different. A new file is saved by typing in the file name. If

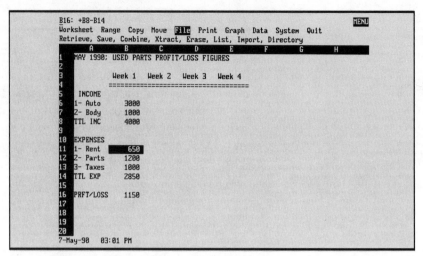

Figure 10.11: *The File commands*

you wish to save an edited worksheet you've saved before, you would press the Enter key at the above prompt to save it under the same name once again. You then will be asked if you want to cancel the save or replace the older version of the worksheet. This is a safety measure to prevent accidentally overwriting the old version in case you need it. To save the old version and keep the new one, just type in a new name.

5. Since your worksheet has never been saved, type **PLMAY90**. If you want to save the file in another subdirectory, type in the new subdirectory name, then the file name.

6. Press the Enter key to save the file. Notice the mode indicator changes to WAIT while the file is being saved. The mode indicator changes back to READY when the saving operation is finished.

*P*rinting the Worksheet on the Network

1-2-3 will send your print requests directly to the local printer port (LPT1, LPT2, or LPT3). This means that if you wish to send your print job to a network printer, you must select the appropriate printer type, the port on which to print, and capture that port to the network printer (not necessarily in that order). (Be sure you've read about capturing in Chapter 8, *Printing Your Documents*, before proceeding.) Usually, the supervisor will place a CAPTURE command in your login script that will automatically capture your printer port, ensuring your print jobs go to the file server print queue and subsequently print on the network printer.

The limited scope of this book prevents us from covering all the variations of network printer configurations, so I recommend you work closely with your supervisor when you begin printing documents on your network. The exercises in this chapter are basic, and assume that your network setup is straightforward.

Selecting the Printer

In order for your document to print properly, you must select the correct printer (when more than one printer is available). One file server can have as many as five printers attached to it. Ask your supervisor what type of printers are in use in your network and which ones are used to print Lotus worksheets. To select the printer you want, follow these steps:

1. Press the Slash key (/). The command line menu appears. The highlight is on Worksheet.

2. Press the Enter key. The Worksheet settings appear. The highlight is on Global.

3. Press the Enter key. The Global format line appears.

4. Move the highlight to Default; the Default menu item allows you to select a new printer.

5. Press the Enter key. The Default Settings menu appears. The highlight is on printer.

6. Press the Enter key. The Printer menu appears. The highlight is on Interface.

7. Press the Enter key. A menu of numbered parallel ports appears.

8. Move the highlight to the port of your choice and press the Enter key. You return to the Printer menu.

9. Move the highlight to Name and press the Enter key. A menu of printer names appears.

10. Move the highlight to the printer you want to print with and press the Enter key. You return to the Printer menu.

11. Press the Esc key four times. You move backward through previous menus until you reach the main command line menu. The highlight is on Worksheet.

You have selected the printer port and printer for your print job. There seems to be an endless number of menu items, but as you gain experience with 1-2-3, you will see how easy it is to move to the menu item you need.

*P*rinting on the Network Printer

Let's print PLMAY90 on the network printer. Before you do, however, let's use the CAPTURE command to make sure your printer port is captured to the network file server. The worksheet should still be on your screen.

1. The command line menu should still be displayed in the control panel. If not, press the slash key (/).

2. Move the highlight to the System command and press the Enter key. You are temporarily placed at a network prompt.

3. Determine the capture options you want (see Chapter 8), and, at the DOS prompt, type **CAPTURE** followed by the capture options you want and press the Enter key. (The Local option enables you to capture the correct parallel port). You will receive a message similar to the following:

   Device LPT1: re-routed to printer 0 on server SYBEX.

   You are returned to a DOS prompt.

4. At the DOS prompt, type **EXIT** and press the Enter key. You are returned to your worksheet and can print to the file server.

Now you're ready to print.

1. Press the slash key (/). The command line menu appears.

2. Move the highlight to the Print command and press the Enter key. The minor print command menu is displayed.

3. The highlight is on Printer. Press Enter. The Printer menu is displayed.

4. The highlight is on Range. Press Enter. You see the prompt

   Enter Print range: B16

B16 is where the pointer is located. You must specify which cells you want printed. Remember, the entire worksheet is huge (256 columns and 8,192 rows); you don't want to try to print an entire worksheet on most printers.

5. Type **A1.E16**. This will print columns A through E and rows 1 through 16. This area includes all the information you entered into the worksheet.

6. Press the Enter key. The Printer menu is displayed.

7. Move the highlight to Go and press the Enter key. The worksheet is sent to the printer queue. Your printed worksheet should look like the one shown in Figure 10.12.

*P*rinting on Your Local Printer

To send a print job to your local printer, the printer port must *not* be captured to the file server. To make certain that the port is not captured, you must exit temporarily to the DOS prompt and use the NetWare ENDCAP command line utility. Let's try it.

1. The command line menu should still be displayed in the control panel. If not, press the slash key (/).

2. Move the highlight to the System command and press the Enter key. You are temporarily placed at a network prompt.

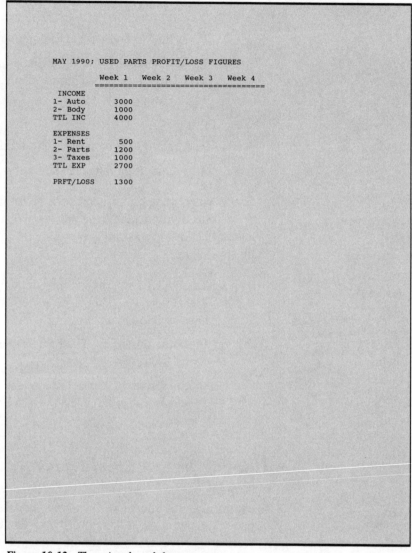

```
MAY 1990; USED PARTS PROFIT/LOSS FIGURES

              Week 1   Week 2   Week 3   Week 4
             =======================================
    INCOME
1- Auto       3000
2- Body       1000
TTL INC       4000

  EXPENSES
1- Rent        500
2- Parts      1200
3- Taxes      1000
TTL EXP       2700

PRFT/LOSS     1300
```

Figure 10.12: *The printed worksheet*

3. Determine the capture options you want to use (see Chapter 8), and at the DOS prompt, type **ENDCAP** and press the Enter key. You will receive a message similar to the following:

   Device LPT1: Set to local mode.

4. At the DOS prompt, type **EXIT** and press the Enter key. You are returned to your worksheet.

Now you can print to your local printer.

1. Press the slash key (/). The command line menu appears.

2. Move the highlight to the Print command and press the Enter key. The minor print command menu is displayed.

3. The highlight is on Printer. Press the Enter key. The Printer menu is displayed.

4. The highlight is on Range. Press Enter. You see the prompt

Enter Print range: B16

B16 is where the pointer is located. You must specify which cells you want printed. Remember, the entire worksheet is huge (256 columns and 8,192 rows); you don't want to try to print an entire worksheet on most printers.

5. Type **A1.E16**. This will print columns A through E and rows 1 through 16. This area includes all the information you entered into the worksheet.

6. Press the Enter key. The Printer menu is displayed.

7. Move the highlight to Go and press the Enter key. The worksheet is sent to the printer queue. Your printed worksheet should look like the one shown in Figure 10.12.

If you attempt to print a job and nothing comes out of the printer, do not keep trying. The print job is out there somewhere, waiting to find a printer that will accept it. New network users frequently try to print a job over and over again without results. They are frustrated and at a total loss about what to do. Suddenly, an unhappy supervisor shows up with several copies of their document. Don't let this happen to you. If you're not sure how your computer is set up to print, ask your supervisor. You'll be glad you did.

Exiting 1-2-3

Exiting 1-2-3 is a simple three-step process.

1. Press the slash key (/). The command line menu appears.

2. Move the highlight to Quit and press the Enter key. You are asked if you really want to quit.

3. Move the highlight to Yes and press the Enter key. You are returned to the DOS prompt.

Before you shut down your workstation or move on to other work, let me show you how to retrieve a worksheet once it is saved.

Retrieving a Saved Worksheet

After you have saved a worksheet, you will need to be able to retrieve it when you need to refer to it or make changes. You use the File command to pull a worksheet out of storage and place it on the screen. You've just saved the sample worksheet under the name PLMAY90.

1. At the DOS prompt, type **123** and press the Enter key. 1-2-3 starts and the worksheet appears on the screen.

2. Press the slash key (/). The command line menu appears.

3. Move the highlight to File and press the Enter key. The File command menu appears.

4. The highlight is on Retrieve. Press the Enter key. The control panel should look similar to that in Figure 10.13. You'll see your own network drive designator and directory path. You are presented with a list of worksheet files that have already been saved.

5. Use the Right Arrow key or the Left Arrow key to scroll through the list of file names. Place the highlight on PLMAY90 and press the Enter key. The worksheet appears on the screen. You can also type in the file name and press the

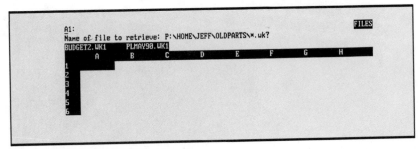

Figure 10.13: *The file retrieve prompt*

Enter key to retrieve the file. If the file you want is not listed in the current directory, type in the path, including the file name, to the correct directory.

Never try to retrieve a file while a worksheet is displayed on the screen. Save the displayed worksheet first or you will replace it with the worksheet you have selected for retrieval.

Summary

In this chapter you learned how to start Lotus 1-2-3, how to construct, edit, save, and retrieve worksheets, and how to print on a network and local printer using the CAPTURE and ENDCAP command line utilities. You should have enough information to get started. If you want more information about 1-2-3, SYBEX offers a wide range of excellent 1-2-3 books for both beginning and advanced users.

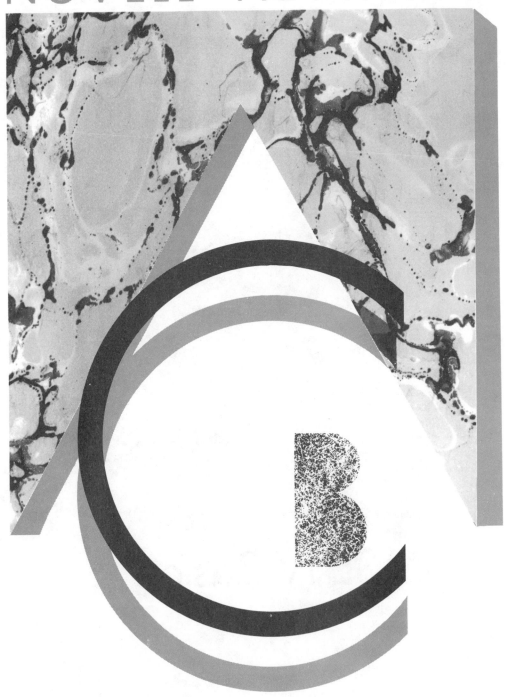

dBASE IV Basics

dBASE IV is a powerful, comprehensive, and sophisticated database management system. With it you can create many different types of databases, make data additions and deletions quickly and easily, search for records with a variety of search criteria, sort data into multiple formats, print mailing labels, generate reports, and, if you work with numerical data, perform various mathematical computations. Quite an impressive array of features.

Of course, it would require a book larger than this one to cover all the features dBASE IV has to offer. This chapter is designed to familiarize the beginning user of dBASE IV with a few of the program's basic operations. You'll learn how to start the program, how to use the Control Center, and how to build a database structure in which to place data. Then you'll actually create and edit a small sample database.

SYBEX publishes several excellent books that offer a comprehensive treatment of the many powerful features of this program. I highly recommend you obtain a copy of one of these books so you can take full advantage of the power of dBASE IV.

Working with dBASE IV on the Network

Like other applications, the dBASE IV program is stored on the file server hard disk in its own subdirectory. The network database files are stored in separate subdirectories where users who have the proper security rights can work with the data. The network supervisor has set up search-drive mappings that allow each workstation user to execute dBASE IV from any subdirectory on the network. This makes it easier for users to find the data files they want, prevents data files from getting mixed in with dBASE IV program files, and ensures users that they will have the correct security rights to do their work.

You will find it helpful if you ask your supervisor to explain your network's organization and to provide you with a diagram of the directory organization so you can see the layout of the directories and subdirectories. Understanding where files and programs are located will make it easier to move about the network. You can become confused and you may become frustrated if you can't effectively maneuver through the directory structure.

Use the MAP command at any DOS prompt to display a list of your drive and search-drive mappings. You should have at least a drive mapping to your home directory and search-drive mappings to the data processing programs that you use. Figure 11.1 shows you a sample search-drive mapping for dBASE IV. (Notice the other search-drive mappings to the WordPerfect and Lotus 1-2-3 subdirectories.)

```
P:\HOME\JEFF>MAP

Drive  A:   maps to a local disk.
Drive  B:   maps to a local disk.
Drive  C:   maps to a local disk.
Drive  D:   maps to a local disk.
Drive  F: = SYBEX/SYS:LOGIN
Drive  P: = SYBEX/SYS:HOME/JEFF

SEARCH1:  = Z:. [SYBEX/SYS:PUBLIC/V3.30]
SEARCH2:  = Y:. [SYBEX/SYS:PUBLIC]
SEARCH3:  = X:. [SYBEX/SYS:MNU]
SEARCH4:  = W:. [SYBEX/SYS:PROG/WP]
SEARCH5:  = V:. [SYBEX/SYS:PROG/123]
SEARCH6:  = U:. [SYBEX/SYS:PROG/DBASEIV]
SEARCH7:  = T:. [SYBEX/SYS:HOME/JEFF]
        -----

P:\HOME\JEFF>_
```

Figure 11.1: *A sample search-drive mapping*

Starting dBASE IV

I will assume you have a search drive mapped to the dBASE IV program subdirectory. In Chapter 7 you created a subdirectory in your home directory called NEWPARTS. Let's create a small database file in this subdirectory. If NEWPARTS no longer exists, create it again with the DOS command MD, which you learned about in Chapter 6. To start dBASE, you'll need to know your username, group, and password for dBASE. This information may be different than that which you use on the network. Ask your supervisor.

1. Turn on your workstation and log in to the network.

2. Change directories to the NEWPARTS subdirectory in your home directory. If you log in to a customized menu, you can exit to a DOS prompt to make this change.

3. At the DOS prompt, type **CAPTURE**. Your LPT1 printer port is now captured to the network printer. (Refer to Chapter 8 for more details on network printing.)

4. At the DOS prompt in the NEWPARTS subdirectory, type **DBASE** and press the Enter key. You will see a licensing agreement. (If dBASE IV is in the protected mode, you will be prompted to enter your group name, your dBASE username, and a password (see Figure 11.2) before you see the licensing agreement. Type in the correct information and press the Enter key.) Press the Enter key at the licensing agreement and the dBASE IV Control Center appears (see Figure 11.3). If you find yourself looking at a blank screen, don't worry; press the F2 function key and the Control Center will appear.

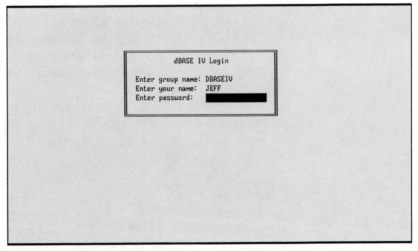

Figure 11.2: *The dBASE IV Login screen*

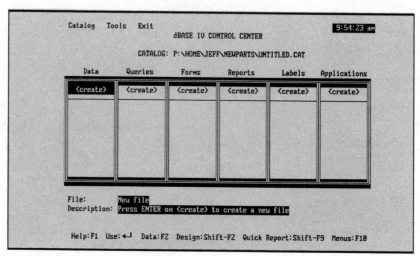

Figure 11.3: The dBASE IV Control Center

A Quick Tour of the Control Center

The operations performed by dBASE IV are initiated from the Control Center. At first, the Control Center looks a little intimidating. To put you at ease, let's look at how the screen is organized. Refer to Figure 11.3 as you read about the following Control Center items.

The *menu bar* is located at the top left of the Control Center. It displays menu options from which you can select the various dBASE IV features.

The *catalog line* is located near the top of the screen. It displays the name of the catalog currently in use. In Figure 11.3, no catalog has been created, so the catalog line reads *UNTITLED.CAT*. A catalog is a grouping of related files.

The six vertical columns in the center of the screen are the *file panels*. They are labeled according to the type of database files you will work on. You may already have several files displayed in the various panels.

The *pointer* is a highlighted bar that is moved by the cursor keys to selected menu options and files. The pointer is highlighting the Data panel in Figure 11.3.

The *file description line*, just below the file panels, lists the name of the currently selected file and a short description of the file's contents.

The *navigation line*, at the bottom of the screen, displays the commands that are available for each option currently selected.

As you create a sample database in the following exercises, you will become familiar with several of these Control Center items.

Creating and Saving a Database Structure

dBASE IV provides the means to organize effectively all the data that goes into your database files. Each piece of raw data—a phone number, name, street number, book title, author's name, and so on—is placed into its own *field*. Several fields of related data are grouped together to create a *record*. Records are compiled into a *database file*, and related database files are organized into a *catalog*. In the following exercises you will create a small phone directory. In the process of doing so, you will become familiar with each of these organizational elements.

Creating a Catalog

Let's suppose you do business with several different companies, and you want to create a separate phone directory for each company. You compile a list of phone numbers for each company and place each list in a different database file. Then, you place all the phone-list database files into one catalog. With this method of organization you can locate important phone numbers that would otherwise become lost in hundreds of other numbers.

Let's create a catalog and call it TELEFONE. During this exercise, and in future exercises, keep an eye on the navigation line at the bottom of the screen. You will receive helpful information on how to proceed with each step.

1. To open the Catalog menu, press F10, the Menu key. The pointer moves to Catalog on the menu line, and the Catalog menu drops down (see Figure 11.4).

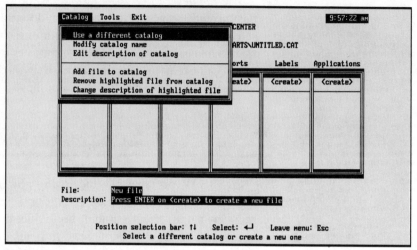

Figure 11.4: *The Catalog menu*

2. The pointer is on the *Use a different catalog* option. Press the Enter key. The Catalog box appears in the upper right corner of the screen. You may see a list of previously created catalogs. Selecting one of these catalogs will display a list of that catalog's files.

3. Be sure the pointer is on *<create>* and press the Enter key. The *Enter name for new catalog* box appears.

4. Type **TELEFONE** and press the Enter key. You are returned to the Control Center. Notice the new catalog name appears in the catalog line (see Figure 11.5). Keep the Control Center on the screen for the next exercise.

A catalog name can consist of up to eight letters or numbers. Do not use punctuation marks or spaces or assign an extension. dBASE assigns the extension .CAT to all catalogs.

*D*efining Data Fields

A data field contains one specific item of data. In the phone book you are creating, the first field will be designated to hold a first name. The second field will be designated to hold a last name; the third, a street address; the fourth, a city; the fifth, a state; the sixth, a zip code; and the seventh, the phone number.

You are poised from the previous exercise to begin defining each of these seven fields for the TELEFONE catalog. Let's begin.

1. The pointer is positioned on *<create>* in the first file panel. Press the Enter key. The Database Design screen appears (see Figure 11.6).

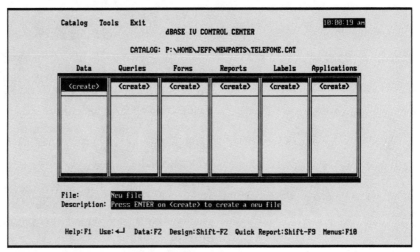

Figure 11.5: *The TELEFONE catalog*

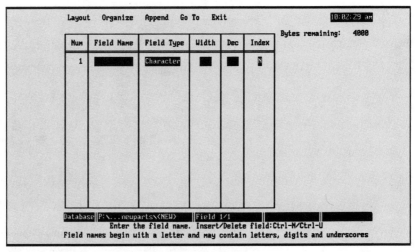

Figure 11.6: *The Database Design screen*

It is in this screen that you will define the fields. The Num column tells you the field number you are working with. The cursor is in the Field Name column. You can enter any name that will identify the type of information to be entered in that field, up to ten characters. We'll name field 1 FIRSTNAME.

2. Type **FIRSTNAME** and press the Enter key. The cursor jumps to the Field Type column. The Field Type column currently indicates that characters will be used in the field, not numerical values. Most of your fields will be Character fields.

3. Press the Enter key. The cursor moves to the Width column. This column is used to define the width of the FIRSTNAME field. Ten spaces is usually plenty of space to enter a person's first name. Longer names can be abbreviated. If you designate too many spaces, you will use up disk storage space unnecessarily.

4. Type **10** and press the Enter key. The cursor jumps past the Dec (for decimal) box because you will not need decimal places with a Character field. Indexing goes beyond the level of this chapter so we'll skip it.

5. Press the Enter key. The cursor is positioned to define the second field. Figure 11.7 shows the seven completed fields.

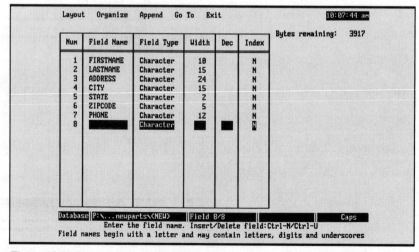

Figure 11.7: *The seven completed fields*

Following the above procedure, enter the remaining field information you see there. When you're finished I'll show you how to save this database file structure.

*S*aving the Database Structure

In the next section you'll enter the specific data for each of the fields in your phone list. But before you can add data, you must save the database structure you just created.

1. Press the F10 key. The Layout menu pops down.

2. Move the pointer to *Save this database file structure*. Press the Enter key. The *Save as* box appears (see Figure 11.8).

3. Type the database name, **TELEFONE**, and press Enter.

The database file structure is now saved, ready to be filled with the data for each individual. dBASE IV will add the extension .DBF to each database file.

Now exit the Database Design screen and return to the Control Center.

4. Press the F10 key. The Layout menu again pops down, this time displaying different options.

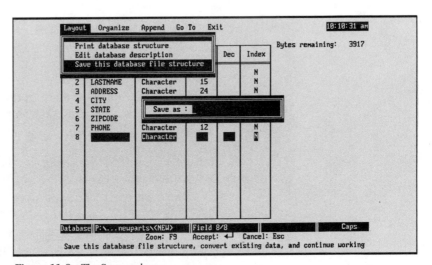

Figure 11.8: *The* Save as *box*

5. Press the Right Arrow key to move the pointer to Exit. Notice how each menu box pops down as the pointer moves from one menu to another.

6. At the Exit menu, the pointer should be on the *Save changes and exit* option. Press the Enter key. You are returned to the Control Center. Notice the TELEFONE database file listed in the Data panel.

Now that you have created the database file structure, it is time to pour data into the fields you have defined. Keep the Control Center on the screen for the next exercise.

*P*lacing Information in the Database Structure

The seven fields created above, when filled with data, combine to form a *record*. Each record you create will contain the name, address, and phone number for each person included in the phone book database. You could compare a record to an index card in the card catalog of your local library. Let's take the database file structure you just constructed and use the Edit screen to create a record.

1. The pointer should be on TELEFONE in the Data panel. Press the Enter key. The box shown in Figure 11.9 appears.

2. Move the pointer to *Display data* and press the Enter key. The Edit screen appears (see Figure 11.10). The seven fields you created appear on the screen. You may now enter specific data into each field and create a record.

3. Starting with FIRSTNAME, type the following information (use the Backspace key to delete any typos), pressing the Enter key after each entry. After you type the information for the STATE, ZIPCODE, and PHONE fields, you'll hear a beep. When you make an entry that uses every assigned space in a field, dBASE will beep at you and automatically jump to the next field.

Barrett
Michaels
112 Elston St.
Pecos
TX
74330
915-555-1432

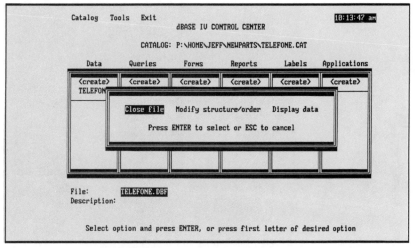

Figure 11.9: *Adding records to the TELEFONE file*

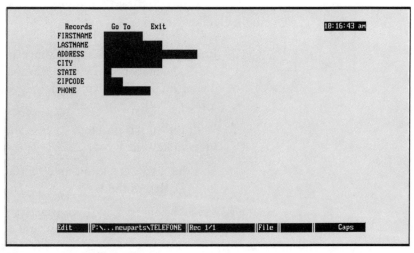

Figure 11.10: *The Edit screen*

When you have completed the first record, dBASE moves to the next blank record.

4. Enter the following information in the next two records:

> **Jacob**
> **Thompson**
> **27 Elfin Way**
> **Monroe**
> **LA**
> **21445**
> **504-555-7789**
>
> **Mary Ann**
> **Mahoney**
> **908 Aspin Dr.**
> **Dedham**
> **MA**
> **02114**
> **617-555-8765**

You are at another blank Edit screen. Remain here and proceed with the next exercise.

*E*diting a Record on the Edit Screen

Let's return to the first record you created and make some changes in the field entries.

1. Press the Up Arrow key to move the cursor backward to the FIRSTNAME field (Barrett) in the first record. You are by default in the Typeover mode; as you type new text, it writes directly over existing text.

2. With the cursor on the *B* in *Barrett*, type **Michael**. Barrett is immediately replaced.

3. Use the arrow keys to move the cursor to the *s* in *Elston* in the ADDRESS field.

4. Press the Insert key (Ins) to activate the Insert mode. Notice the Ins indicator in the lower-right corner of the screen.

5. Type **li**. Elston becomes Elliston as the letters *li* are inserted into the middle of the word and the rest of the line is pushed to the right. Your Edit screen should look like that in Figure 11.11.

6. Press the Insert key to return to the Typeover mode.

*E*xiting the Edit Screen

You have created and edited three records. Your database is more than just a structure; it now contains data. Let's exit from the Edit screen back to the Control Center.

1. Press the Down Arrow key until you reach the end of the last record and see the following prompt at the bottom of the Edit screen:

    === > **Add new records? (Y/N)**

2. Press Y for Yes and a blank set of fields appears.

3. Press the Enter key. You are returned to the Control Center. Keep it on your screen and move to the next exercise.

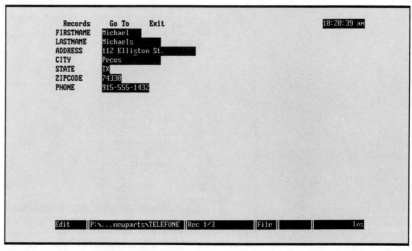

Figure 11.11: A modified record

Working with the Database

This section shows you some basic ways to work with a database once you have created it. You will want to look frequently at the status of your databases and update them as needed. In this section I'll show you how to display a listing of your database records, update them, and delete out-of-date entries.

Viewing a List of Records

On the Edit screen you are limited to viewing one record at a time. With the Browse mode, however, you can view a screen full of records. Let's use the Data key (F2) and look at the three records listed in the TELEFONE database file.

1. Move the pointer to the TELEFONE file name in the Data file panel.

2. Press the F2 key. The Browse screen appears (Figure 11.12). If the Edit screen appears, press F2 again.

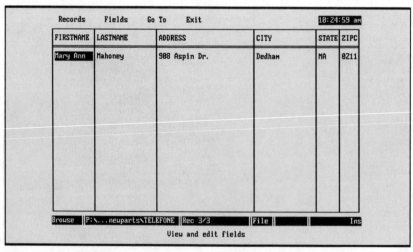

Figure 11.12: The Browse screen

The records are listed down the page and the field information for each record is displayed across the page in seven columns. (If you see only one record, press the Up Arrow key to pull the other records into view. Also, the screen is only wide enough to see five complete columns, so you have to move the cursor across the screen to reveal the hidden columns.)

Editing and Adding Records in the Browse Screen

You can edit existing records and add new records directly on the Browse screen. To edit an existing record, simply move the cursor to the field that needs changing and type in the correct information. Let's try it.

1. Press the End key. The pointer moves to the last field, PHONE, in the Michael Michaels record.

2. Type

   915-555-3355

   The old phone number is overwritten, dBASE IV beeps, and the pointer is moved to the first field of the next record. (Remember, whenever you enter information in the last space of a field, dBASE IV beeps, and the cursor is moved to the next field.)

3. Press the Tab key three times. The pointer returns to the CITY field (Monroe) in the second record.

4. Type **Ruston**. Monroe is overwritten by Ruston.

5. Press Shift-Tab three times. The pointer returns to the FIRST-NAME field of the second record.

Now add a new record to the database.

6. Press the Down Arrow key once, then press the Tab key seven times until the following message appears at the bottom of the Browse screen:

   = = = > Add new records? (Y/N)

7. Press Y for Yes. The pointer moves to the FIRSTNAME field of the next blank record.

8. Type in this record, pressing Enter after each entry.

> April
> Jones
> 223 Holton Lane
> Los Angeles
> CA
> 90021
> 213-555-6117

The pointer moves to the next blank record and waits for the next record to be entered (see Figure 11.13). Keep the Browse screen on your monitor for the next exercise.

*M*arking and Deleting Records

It is important that outdated records be deleted regularly. They take up valuable disk space, increase the time it takes to perform database operations, and can interfere with other records during certain database processes. It's also expensive to send mailings to outdated addresses or to make long-distance phone calls to the wrong people.

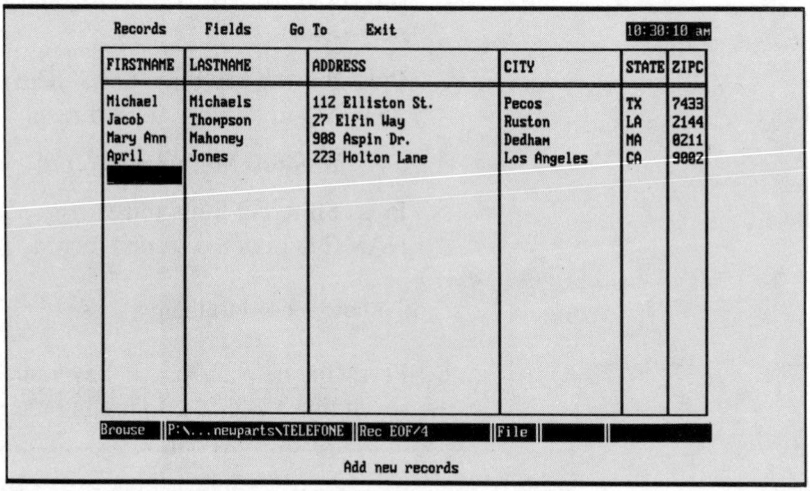

Records	Fields	Go To	Exit		10:30:10 am
FIRSTNAME	LASTNAME	ADDRESS	CITY	STATE	ZIPC
Michael	Michaels	112 Elliston St.	Pecos	TX	7433
Jacob	Thompson	27 Elfin Way	Ruston	LA	2144
Mary Ann	Mahoney	988 Aspin Dr.	Dedham	MA	8211
April	Jones	223 Holton Lane	Los Angeles	CA	9882

Browse P:\...newparts\TELEFONE Rec EOF/4 File

Add new records

Figure 11.13: *The edited Browse screen*

Marking Records for Deletion

Before you delete a record it must be *marked* for deletion. You can mark one or more records at a time. In this exercise, let's mark two records for deletion using a different method for each.

1. Move the pointer to the FIRSTNAME field of the second record (Jacob).

2. Press F10. The Records menu appears (see Figure 11.14).

3. Move the pointer to the *Mark record for deletion* option and press the Enter key. The record is marked. Notice the Del prompt in the lower-right corner of your screen.

4. Move the pointer to the FIRSTNAME field of the fourth record (April).

5. Mark this record by pressing Ctrl-U. Note the Del prompt in the lower-right corner of the screen; the record is marked for deletion.

What happens if you mark the wrong record for deletion? The next section tells you how to unmark the record.

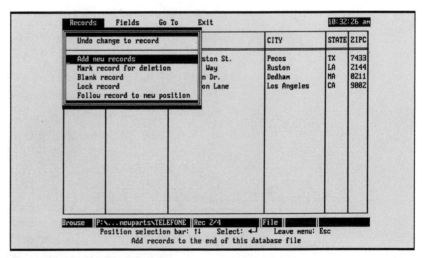

Figure 11.14: *The Records menu*

Unmarking a Record for Deletion

To unmark a record that has been marked for deletion, you place the pointer on the marked record and press the F10 key. The Records menu appears with the *Clear deletion mark* option highlighted. Press the Enter key and the Del prompt in the lower-right corner of the screen disappears, indicating the record is no longer marked for deletion. As in the previous exercise on marking a record for deletion, you can also use Ctrl-U to unmark a record. Simply place the pointer on the marked record and press Ctrl-U. The Del prompt once again disappears.

Deleting Marked Records

When you delete records from the database file, dBASE IV shifts the remaining records to occupy the space on the disk made vacant by the deleted records. This process is referred to as *packing the database*. Let's delete the two files you marked previously. Mark them again, if you unmarked them in the last section.

1. Exit the Browse screen (F10, Exit menu) and return to the Control Center.

2. Press Shift-F2. The Database Design screen appears and the Organize menu pops down.

3. Move the pointer to *Erase marked records*. Press the Enter key. The box in Figure 11.15 appears.

4. Select Yes and press the Enter key. You return to the Database Design screen, and the records are deleted from the database.

5. To exit, press the F10 key, move to the Exit menu, and press the Enter key. You return to the Control Center.

*P*rinting a Quick Report

Most printing procedures with dBASE IV are beyond the scope of this chapter. However, dBASE IV has a quick method of printing out a report of a file's records. Before you can print on the network, however, you must make certain your print jobs go to the correct printer.

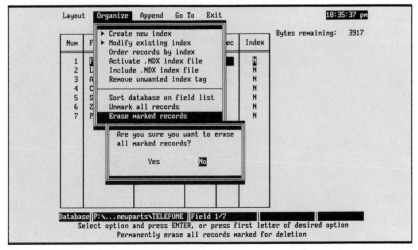

Figure 11.15: *Deleting marked files*

If you haven't already done so, I recommend you read Chapter 8 for a discussion of the CAPTURE and ENDCAP commands.

In the first exercise in this chapter, prior to starting dBASE IV, you used the CAPTURE command to direct your print jobs to the network printer. Let's print a copy of your TELEFONE database.

1. Move the pointer to the TELEFONE file name in the Data panel. Press Shift-F9. The Print box appears.

2. With the *Begin printing* option highlighted, press the Enter key. Your print job is sent to the network printer. Your printed document will look similar to the example Figure 11.16.

*E*xiting dBASE IV

Exiting dBASE IV after your work is finished is very easy. Follow these steps.

1. Return to the Control Center.
2. Press F10 and move to the Exit menu.

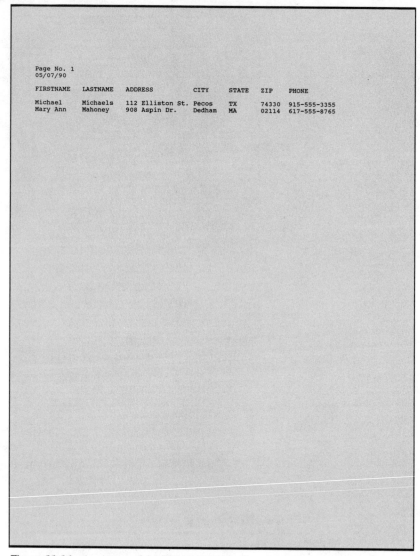

```
Page No. 1
05/07/90

FIRSTNAME   LASTNAME   ADDRESS            CITY      STATE   ZIP     PHONE

Michael     Michaels   112 Elliston St.   Pecos     TX      74330   915-555-3355
Mary Ann    Mahoney    908 Aspin Dr.      Dedham    MA      02114   617-555-8765
```

Figure 11.16: A printout of the TELEFONE file

3. Move the pointer to *Quit to DOS* and press the Enter key. You exit to a DOS prompt.

4. If you need to use your local printer, type **ENDCAP** at the DOS prompt and capturing will be turned off.

*S*ummary

This chapter on dBASE IV has been necessarily brief. You have learned how to start dBASE IV, move around the Control Center, work with menus, create a catalog and database structure, fill the structure with records, edit them, and print out a quick report. You are now prepared to delve into some of the more powerful features that are packed into the program.

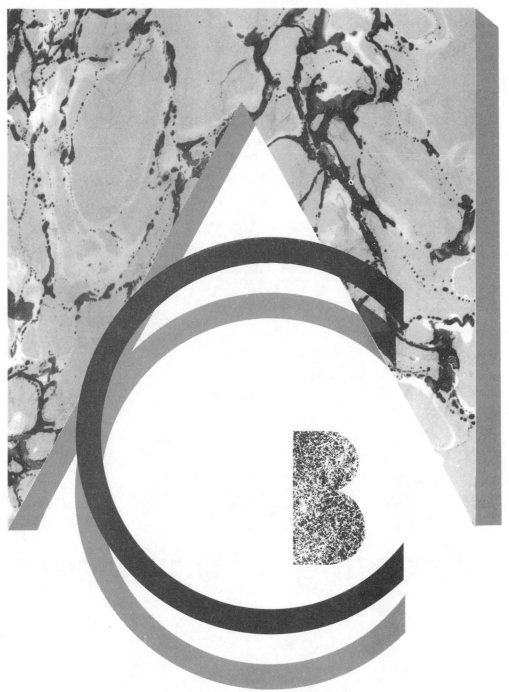

Creating a Login Script

If you are new to working with the NetWare networking system, I suggest you read the first six chapters of this book before attempting to follow the instructions in this appendix. Otherwise, much of what you read here will have little meaning to you.

A login script contains a set of instructions that the NetWare operating system reads and executes whenever you log in to the network. There are two types of login scripts, system and personal. The network supervisor controls the system login script. This script primarily contains drive mappings and search-drive mappings that affect all the network workstations. These drive mappings may be modified only by someone with supervisory rights over the network. Personal login scripts are often initially created by the supervisor, but may be created or changed by the individual user. When you log in to the network, the system login script is executed first, followed by your personal login script.

Chapter 6 contains instructions for mapping network drives to directories. These drive mappings are only active during that particular login period. Personal login scripts are used to save these drive mappings permanently so you don't have to map the same drives every time you log in.

This appendix shows you how to open your login script using the SYSCON menu utility, make additions, deletions, or additions to your drive mappings, and exit SYSCON. You will also learn how to place a short message in the login script using the WRITE command.

*O*pening Your Login Script

There are a total of 26 drive letters available to each workstation, drives A through Z; the first five drives, A through E, are usually reserved for local drives (there may be fewer, depending on the version of DOS you are using). You cannot map to a local drive, only to a network drive. Network drives use the remaining drive designations, F through Z.

Before you can make a personal drive mapping permanent, you must start the SYSCON menu utility and move to the login script screen. In these exercises, I will illustrate this procedure by showing you examples of the login script for user JEFF.

1. If you haven't already done so, log in to the network. Move to your home directory if the system login script has not automatically placed you there.

2. At the DOS prompt, type **SYSCON** and press the Enter key. The Available Topics menu appears.

3. Move the highlight to User Information and press the Enter key. The User Names list appears.

4. Move the highlight to your username and press the Enter key. The User Information menu appears (see Figure A.1).

5. Move the highlight to Login Script and press the Enter key. Your personal login script screen is displayed (see Figure A.2).

You may or may not have information recorded on the screen. If you do, don't modify it until you check with your supervisor. You don't want to harm any important commands your supervisor has set up for you.

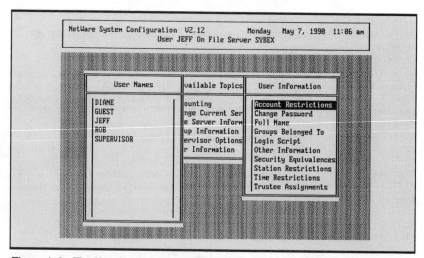

Figure A.1: *The User Information menu*

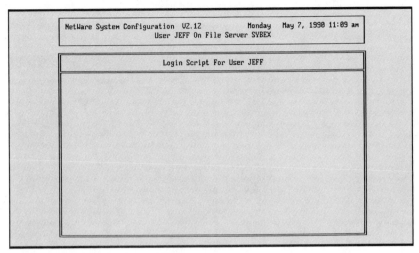

Figure A.2: The Login Script screen

You can add a drive mapping anywhere in the login script, but it is easier to view your drive mapping list if you keep all the mappings together. Let's add a new mapping to your login script.

6. If your script already has mappings, insert a blank line after your present mappings. If you have no mappings, insert a blank line anywhere in the script.

7. Use the following format to enter a drive mapping:

   MAP *drive letter*: = *server/volume:directory/subdirectory*

   Substitute your own network drive, server name, and volume, directory, and subdirectory names. Your new drive map entry should have the same format as the one shown in Figure A.3.

Figure A.3 shows you an example of a drive mapping to the NEW-PARTS subdirectory in user Jeff's personal login script. The network drive is G; the server name is SYBEX; the volume name is SYS; the directory is HOME; the first subdirectory is JEFF; and the second subdirectory is NEWPARTS.

From now on, when Jeff logs in, this drive mapping will be listed along with the drive mappings the supervisor may have set up in the system login script.

Keep your login script on your screen for the next exercise.

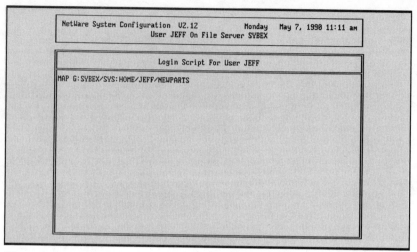

```
NetWare System Configuration  V2.12           Monday   May 7, 1990 11:11 am
                      User JEFF On File Server SYBEX

                       Login Script For User JEFF
MAP G:SYBEX/SYS:HOME/JEFF/NEWPARTS
```

Figure A.3: A drive map entry

Writing a Message in the Login Script

NetWare lets you send yourself a message when you log in to the network. This message can be a simple greeting, display the date and time, or remind you of important meetings. You use the WRITE command to place the message in the login script. You can enter both textual information and variable identifiers. *Variable identifiers* are commands that read variable information generated in other areas of the computer, such as the current date and time, the day of the week, and the current user's login name. You enter this information into your login script by typing in the command for a particular identifier. Table A.1 lists commands for the most common variable information.

Let's use the WRITE command to add a short message to your login script.

1. You should still have your login script on your monitor from the last exercise. Move the cursor to the end of the login script and start a new line.

2. Type

   WRITE "Good "; GREETING_TIME; ", "; LOGIN_NAME

Table A.1: *A Partial List of Variable Identifiers and Their Functions*

Variable Identifier	Screen Display
HOUR	Hour of the day or night (1 to 12)
HOUR24	Hour of the day or night in 24-hour clock format (01 to 24)
MINUTE	Minutes (00 to 59)
SECOND	Seconds (00 to 59)
AM_PM	Daytime or night time (AM or PM)
MONTH	Month number (01 to 12)
MONTH_NAME	Month name
YEAR	Year in four digits
SHORT_YEAR	Year in last two digits only
DAY_OF_WEEK	Day name
LOGIN_NAME	User's login name
FULL_NAME	User's full name as listed in SYSCON
GREETING_TIME	Specifies morning, afternoon, or evening

If user Jeff logs in to the network in the morning, he will see *Good morning, JEFF*. If he logs in during the evening, the message will read *Good evening, JEFF*.

Textual information is always enclosed in quotation marks. Notice the extra space included after the word *Good* and the comma, both are textual information and both are enclosed in quotation marks. These spaces are needed to separate the variable identifiers representing the words *morning* and *JEFF* from the word *Good* and the comma. Without them, the greeting would be displayed as *Goodmorning,JEFF*.

3. To exit from SYSCON and save the login script, press the Escape key once. The Save Login Script box appears.

4. The highlight is on Yes. Press the Enter key.

5. Press the Escape key three times. At the Exit SYSCON box, select Yes and press Enter. You are returned to a DOS prompt.

6. To check the results of these additions to the login script, log out of the network and log back in. You should see the new drive mapping listed in the drive map listing, followed by the greeting. Figure A.4 shows you user JEFF's new login information. Yours should look similar.

Modifying your personal login script can be very helpful, as well as add a nice personal touch to your login display.

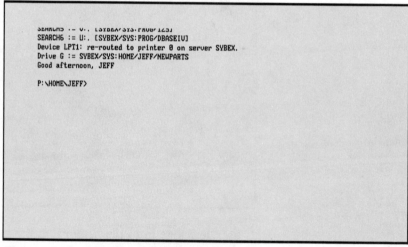

Figure A.4: *User JEFF's new login information*

Glossary

address: An identifying number for a location in computer memory. Also a unique number that identifies a particular network or network station.

application: A software program or program package that makes calls to the operating system and manipulates data files, thus allowing a user to perform a specific job (such as accounting or word processing).

archive: To back up data files. *See also* back up.

ASCII (American Standard Code for Information Interchange): A standard character set that uses a seven-bit code to create 128 characters. IBM PC-compatible computers use an extended ASCII character set, which adds an eighth bit to the code, doubling the number of characters to 256. Each bit pattern determines the appearance of a character. ASCII characters form the computer's text display and control such features as backspace, line feed, carriage return, etc.

attach: To access a file server; particularly to access additional file servers after having already logged in to one file server. The term also means to connect components, often by cable.

attributes: *See* file attributes.

back up (verb): To copy a file, directory, or volume onto another storage device so that the data may be retrieved if the original source is accidentally corrupted or destroyed. Also known as *archiving*.

backup (noun): A stored copy of a file, directory, or volume preserved as a safeguard in case the original is accidentally corrupted or destroyed.

This glossary was excerpted from *Novell Guide to SFT/Advanced NetWare Manuals—NetWare* © 1988 with permission from Novell, Inc.

banner: The first page of a printout that gives information about the file being printed. The banner page usually identifies the user who printed the file, the name of the file, the directory the file came from, the connection number of the workstation the file was printed from, the print queue, the file server, and the date and time the file was printed.

bit: A binary digit; must be either a 0 or a 1. It is the smallest unit of information and indicates one of two states—"off" (0) or "on" (1).

boot (boot up):   To load a computer's operating system into RAM. After the operating system has been booted, applications can be loaded into the computer. *See also* cold boot; remote reset; and warm boot.

bridge: A software and hardware connection between two networks, usually of similar design. A NetWare bridge can connect networks that use different kinds of network interface boards or transmission media, as long as both sides of the connection use the IPX protocol. There are two types of NetWare bridges; internal and external. If a bridge is located in a file server, it is an internal bridge. If a bridge is located in a workstation, it is an external bridge. *See also* internetwork.

buffer: A storage area in RAM where data that is being transferred may be stored temporarily. Data is placed in buffers when the devices handing the data process it at different speeds. For example, a printer may not be able to process information as fast as a file server can send it. Any information the printer is receiving but cannot process immediately is placed in a buffer until the information can be processed.

byte: Usually the eight bits that represent a character in binary.

central processing unit: *See* CPU.

character: A unit of information that is usually composed of six, seven, or eight bits. Also, the figure that designates each unit of information.

character set: The group of characters a computer can recognize and process. PC-compatible computers use an extended ASCII character set.

coaxial cable: A connecting cable consisting of two insulating layers and two conductors. A central conductor wire is surrounded by the first layer of insulation. An outer shielding conductor is laid over this insulation and then covered with the second layer of insulation.

cold boot: To reload a computer's operating system by turning the computer's power off and then back on. (If a computer has a reset switch, a cold boot can be performed without turning the power off and on.) *See also* boot.

COM1, COM2:

command: An instruction, entered by a user, that tells the computer to perform a specific task.

configuration, hardware:

1) The equipment used on a network (file servers, workstations, printers, cables, network interface boards, bridges, etc.), and the way it is connected—the physical layout of the network.

2) The specific type of hardware installed in or attached to the computer itself, such as disk subsystems, network interface boards, memory boards, printer boards, etc.

3) A specific set of parameters selected for a board.

configuration, software: The procedure that prepares software programs to run on the computer's specific hardware, operating system, memory capacity, peripherals, etc.

connection number: A number assigned to any station that attaches to a file server; it may be a different number each time a station attaches. The file server's operating system uses connection numbers to control each station's communication with other stations. You can determine your connection number by executing the WHOAMI or USERLIST command line utilities.

console: The monitor and keyboard from which you actually view and control server activity. At the console, you can type in commands to control printers and disk drives, send messages, set the file server clock, shut down the file server, and view file server information.

CPU (central processing unit): The circuit board or chip that controls all activity within a computer system—receiving information, acting on it, and then sending it somewhere else.

crash: A slang term that means hardware or software has stopped working properly.

current directory: The directory you are working in; your default directory.

current drive: *See* default drive.

cylinder (hard disk): Distinct, concentric storage areas on a hard disk (roughly corresponding to tracks on a floppy diskette). Generally, the more cylinders a hard disk has, the greater its storage capacity.

database: On a network, a collection of data organized and stored on disk by network users, usually through use of a special application program.

dedicated file server: *See* file server.

default: A value or option that is chosen automatically when no other value is specified. For example, if a word processing program has a preset page length, it is called the default page length.

default drive: The drive that a workstation is currently using. The drive prompt (A>, C>, etc.) identifies the default drive letter.

default server: The file server to which your default drive is mapped. In other words, the drive you are currently using is mapped to a particular file server; therefore, that file server is your default server. Any commands that you enter will be directed automatically to the default server *unless you specify otherwise.*

destination: The network station, directory, drive, printer, file, etc., to which data is sent.

directory:

1) A logical portion of disk space that is named. Users create directories and assign them names. A directory may be part of another directory, and may itself contain several other directories. The different "levels" of directories on any disk form a hierarchical "directory structure." Directories contain files that are grouped together conveniently.

2) The list of files that are contained in a directory. This list is displayed when the NetWare directory command NDIR, or the DOS directory command DIR, is issued at any directory level.

directory name (path): A name that both identifies a directory and reflects its position within a directory structure. On a network, the full directory name lists the name of the file server, the volume, and each subdirectory leading down to the directory you need to access. The directory name is also called the directory path.

directory rights: Restrictions specific to a directory that regulate trustee activity within it. Directory rights are limited to a single directory and do not extend down through the directory structure. *See also* maximum rights mask.

directory structure: The different levels of directories (parent directories, subdirectories, etc.) organized to form a hierarchy. *See also* directory name.

disk: A magnetically encoded storage medium in the form of a plate (also called a platter). For example, three types of disks are used with personal computers: hard, flexible, and floppy. Hard disks use a metallic base and are usually installed within a computer or disk subsystem. (In some cases the storage media may be removable.) Floppy and flexible disks (called diskettes) use a polyester base and are always removable. *See also* disk drive.

disk drive: A storage device that allows users to read, write, and delete data. A disk drive can be internal (built into the computer) or external (attached as a peripheral to the computer). The operation of the disk drive is regulated by a disk controller. *See also* drive; floppy disk drive; and hard disk.

disk mirroring: An SFT NetWare method of safeguarding data in which the same data is copied to two hard disks on the same channel. If one of the disks fails, the data on the other disk is safe. Because the two disks are on the same channel, mirroring provides only limited data protection—a failure anywhere along the channel could shut down both disks and data would be lost.

disk operating system: *See* DOS.

disk subsystem: An external unit that attaches to the file server and many contain hard disk drives, a tape drive, or both. The disk subsystem gives the file server more storage capacity. A disk channel can accommodate up to eight disk subsystems.

diskette (floppy): *See* disk.

DOS (disk operating system): An operating system for individual personal computers that is stored on disk. *See also* operating system.

DOS text file: A file made up of ASCII characters.

drive:

1) A storage device that data is written to and read from, such as a disk drive or tape drive (*physical* drive). A drive that is physically attached to a workstation is called a *local* drive. *See also* disk drive.

2) An identification for a specific directory located on a disk drive. For example a *network* (*logical*) drive reads information from a specified directory on the network, rather than from a local disk.

drive letter: A letter that can represent a local drive, a network drive, or a logical drive.

drive mapping: *See* map.

dynamic memory: A form of memory that requires a continual rewriting of all stored information. A continuous electrical current is necessary to maintain dynamic memory. A common example is dynamic RAM: all data is lost when the power supply is turned off.

effective rights: The rights a user may actually exercise in a given directory. Two factors determine effective rights:

1) Trustee rights granted to a particular user;

2) Directory rights specified in the directory's maximum rights mask.

Since directory rights always take precedence over trustee rights, any trustee right not specifically denied in the maximum rights mask is an effective right.

expansion slot: A space within a personal computer where add-on boards can be connected to the data bus.

extended memory: In a personal computer running DOS, extended memory is memory above the 1MB address range. Normally, this memory is available to DOS only as a virtual disk (memory that is treated as though it were a disk drive). The NetWare operating system also uses this memory.

FAT: *See* file allocation table.

file: A collection of data stored as one unit and given a filename. A file may contain many separate items (for example, a list of names and addresses), or it may contain continuous text (such as a letter). A file can be stored and saved on a disk or magnetic tape, and then retrieved later to be viewed or changed.

file allocation table (FAT): An index on a disk that records the disk location of all the parts of a file.

file attributes: Designations that regulate how a file may be handled on the network. For example, a file can be assigned the attributes "Shareable" and "Read/Only." "Shareable" means that more than one user may access the file at the same time; "Read/Only" means that users can read the file, but they cannot alter it.

file server (dedicated and nondedicated): A computer that controls all network activity. The NetWare operating system is loaded into the file server, and all modems and shareable devices (disk subsystems, printers, etc.) are attached to it. The file server controls all access to shared devices and the system security; it also monitors station-to-station communications. A *dedicated* file server can be used only as a file server while it is on the network. A *nondedicated* file server can be used simultaneously as a file server and a workstation.

file sharing: An important feature of networking that allows more than one user to access the same file at the same time. *See also* multiuser network; file attributes.

flag: *See* option.

floppy disk drive: A disk drive that reads from and writes to a floppy diskette. *See also* disk drive.

floppy diskette: Another name for a flexible diskette, a removable magnetic storage medium. *See also* disk.

form: In a printer command, the design or shape of the printing surface, such as letter-size paper, labels, continuous-feed paper, etc.

format (noun): The logical or physical arrangement of the tracks and sectors on a floppy diskette or a hard disk. To be usable, a disk must be formatted so that the tracks and sectors are laid out in a manner compatible with the disk driver in use.

format (verb): To prepare a disk or diskette, dividing it into sectors so that it is ready to receive data.

group access: A method of granting identical rights to several users at the same time so they can all access the same directories. Rather than repetitively assigning each individual user the same rights, the network supervisor can make each user a member of the same group, then grant that group the needed rights.

hard copy: A paper printout. It is "hard" because it is a tangible copy rather than simply a screen display.

hard disk: A high-capacity magnetic storage device that allows a user to write, read, and erase data. Hard disks may be network disks, or they may be attached locally to workstations. *See also* disk drive.

hardware: Physical equipment. All of the electronic and mechanical components of a network, such as personal computers, network interface boards, disk drives, hub devices, cables, etc.

head: The mechanism in a drive that writes data to and retrieves data from an electronic medium. For example, when a hard disk is operating, the hard disk head floats on a cushion of air just above the surface of the rotating disk while it writes data to and reads data from the disk.

hierarchy: Refers to a directory structure made up of different levels in which some directories are parts of others and the entire structure is organized in a branching, tree-like form.

home directory: A network directory that the network supervisor creates specifically for you. The supervisor may include a drive mapping to your home directory in your login script.

host: A computer, attached to a network, that provides services to another computer beyond simply storing and forwarding information. Mainframes, minicomputers, and file servers are sometimes called hosts, but the term is often used more broadly. For example, the network station that a remote caller takes over and controls is referred to as the host.

Hz (hertz): Unit of measurement for electrical frequency representing the number of cycles per second. One hertz equals one cycle per second.

identifier: Words used in a login script command to represent information that may vary each time a user logs in. When an identifier appears in the login script, the current value for the information is automatically supplied. Some examples of identifiers are HOUR, DAY_OF_WEEK, LOGIN_NAME, STATION.

internetwork (internet): Two or more networks connected by an internal or external bridge. Users on an internetwork may use the resources (files, printers, disk drives, etc.) of all connected networks. *See also* bridge.

Internetwork Packet Exchange: *See* IPX.

IPX (Internetwork Packet Exchange): A protocol that allows the exchange of message packets on an internetwork. With IPX, applications running on a NetWare workstation can use the NetWare network drivers to communicate directly with other workstations, servers, or devices on the internetwork. IPX is based on Xerox Corporation's Internetwork Packet Protocol.

KB (kilobyte): A unit of measure for memory or disk storage capacity; two to the tenth power (1024) bytes.

LAN (local area network): *See* network.

local area network (LAN): *See* network.

local disk: A disk that is attached to a workstation but is not part of the network. A local disk can be accessed only by the workstation to which it is attached. It does not contain network files and cannot be accessed by other stations on the network.

log in (verb): To gain access to the network. Logging in to the network involves executing a login script and establishing yourself as a user.

login (noun): The process of accessing the network.

login script: The set of instructions that directs your workstation to perform specific actions when you log in to the network. The network supervisor can create a system-wide login script (which is the same for all users on the network) that instructs all workstations to perform the same actions upon login. Your individual login script executes after the system-wide login script; it specifies your individual drive mappings. (You do not access a second login script when you attach to an additional file server.)

LPT1: The primary printer port of a workstation. *See also* parallel port.

map or mapping: To assign a drive letter to a chosen directory path (on a particular volume of a particular file server). This is done with the MAP command line utility. For example, if you map (assign) drive F to the directory SYS:ACCOUNT/RECEIVE, you will access that directory every time you type **F:** at the DOS prompt.

maximum rights mask: A feature of directory security that controls the rights that all trustees may exercise in one directory. If a particular right is removed from a directory's rights mask, no user (other than SUPERVISOR) will be able to exercise that right *in that directory* or its subdirectories, even if the user has that *trustee* right. *See also* directory rights; effective rights; and trustee rights.

MB (megabyte): A unit of measure for memory or disk storage capacity. Two to the twentieth power (1,048,576) bytes.

Mbps: Megabits per second (one million bits per second).

memory: One of the essential components of a computer's central processing unit. Memory is the area where information and programs are actively processed. *See also* RAM; ROM.

memory board: An add-on board designed to increase the amount of RAM within a personal computer.

MHz (megahertz): One million cycles per second. *See also* Hz.

microprocessor: A chip that acts as the central processing unit inside a personal computer.

modem (MODulator/DEModulator): A hardware device that sends data via telephone lines from one computer device to another or to a network resource, such as a file server.

monitor: Any computer display screen.

Monitor Display: A formatted screen display that may be displayed on any console screen by entering the MONITOR console command. The Monitor Display shows file server activity and allows you to manage server resources.

multiserver network: A single network that has two or more file servers operating on it. On a multiserver network, users may access files from any file server to which they are attached (if they have access rights). A multiserver network should not be confused with an internetwork (two or more networks linked together through a bridge).

multiuser network: An operating system that allows several users (at separate workstations) to share a system's resources, such as processing power, data, printers, disks, etc. The NetWare operating system is a multiuser system.

NetWare: Networking software products made by Novell, Inc. NetWare, a registered trademark, generally refers to the Novell network operating system and its related software.

NetWare operating system: The operating system developed by Novell, Inc. The NetWare operating system is loaded into the file server when the file server is booted; it controls all system resources and the way information is processed on the entire network or internetwork.

NetWare shell: The special NetWare program that is loaded into the memory of each workstation. It is called a shell because it builds itself around DOS and intercepts the workstation's network requests, rerouting them to a NetWare file server. Shells can be configured for several different types of workstations running different versions of DOS so that all may operate on the same NetWare network.

network: A group of computers that can communicate with each other, share peripherals (such as hard disks and printers), and, if desired, access remote hosts or other networks. A NetWare network consists of one or more file servers, workstations, and peripherals. NetWare network users may share the same files (both data and program files), send messages directly between individual workstations, and protect files by means of an extensive security system.

network communication: Data transmission between network stations. Requests for services and data are passed from one network station to another through a communication medium such as cabling.

network console: *See* console.

network disk: A hard disk controlled by the file server.

network interface board: A circuit board installed in each network station to allow stations to communicate with each other and with the file server.

network operator: A user given special responsibilities on the network. For example, a print queue operator is a user who is allowed to manage printer queues, changing the position of jobs in the queue or deleting them altogether.

network station: Any personal computer (or other device) connected to a network by means of a network interface board and some communication medium. A network station can be a workstation, bridge, or server.

node: Any network station.

nondedicated file server: *See* file server.

operating system: The software that controls the computer. The operating system controls the way applications utilize the computer and its attached peripherals. *See also* NetWare operating system; DOS.

option: One of several variables that can appear in a command format. Option indicates that one or more modifications may be included when entering the command.

parallel port: A printer interface that allows data to be transmitted a byte at a time, with all eight bits moving in parallel. *See also* LPT1.

parameter: In command format, a value or group of values that restricts or determines the specific form of the command. A command may have several parameters, and each parameter may contain numerous items from which to choose. For example, a particular command may allow you to specify such parameters as which drive, which directory, which filename to use, etc. If a parameter can have more than one value, it is called a variable.

parent directory: The directory immediately above any subdirectory. For example, SYS:ACCOUNT would be the parent directory of the subdirectory SYS:ACCOUNT/RECEIVE.

partition: A portion of a hard disk's physical storage space that is allocated to an operating system (NetWare, DOS, etc.). Once created, a partition belongs exclusively to the specified operating system; no other operating system can access that area.

password protection: A security feature that requires a user to enter a correct password before being allowed to log in to the network.

path: One of several variables that can appear in a command format. Path represents the designation of a directory path starting from the drive and volume to the directory or subdirectory level. It does not include the filename.

peripheral: A physical drive (such as a printer or disk subsystem) that is externally attached to a workstation or to the network.

port (verb): To move from one environment to another.

port, hardware (noun): A connecting component that allows a microprocessor to communicate with a compatible peripheral. *See also* parallel port; serial port.

print device: A printer, plotter, or other peripheral used to create hard copy.

print job configuration: The characteristics that determine how a job is printed. Some of the factors may include the mode, the form, the number of copies, and the particular printer that will be used.

prompt: A character or message (from the software) that appears on the display screen and requires a response from the user. "D>" and "Enter your password:" are examples of prompts.

public access: A security condition that gives *all* users access rights to a particular directory. For example, all users must be able to access NetWare utilities. Therefore, NetWare utilities are usually placed in a directory (named SYS:PUBLIC) that has public access rights; in other words, all users have the right to open, read, and search for files in that directory.

queue: A data-handling structure that stores requests (such as print jobs) in the order they are received while they await servicing. The first request that arrives is the first to be handled. Later requests are placed in the queue and must "wait in line" to be processed unless assigned a higher priority.

RAM (random access memory): A type of storage in which each byte of information has a particular address, independent of all other bytes, and can be accessed in any order. This type of access is very fast. RAM is usually temporary memory, the data stored in RAM being lost when the computer is turned off. *See also* ROM.

random access memory: *See* RAM.

read: To retrieve data from a storage medium. For example, when a computer transfers data from a hard disk drive into its memory, the computer is "reading" the data from the hard disk.

read-only: A type of data security that protects files. If a file is flagged Read-Only, a user can access the data in the file but cannot change it. *See also* file attributes.

read-only memory: *See* ROM.

record: A collection of related information that is treated as one unit within a file.

record locking: An important feature of the NetWare operating system that prevents different users from gaining simultaneous access to the same record in a shared file, thus preventing overlapping disk writes and ensuring data integrity.

remote: A connection between a LAN and a workstation or network, often using telephone lines. A remote connection allows data to be sent and received across distances greater than those allowed by normal cabling.

remote reset: A feature that enables a workstation to boot from the network, without using a local disk. *See also* boot.

remote workstation: A terminal or personal computer that is not part of the LAN, but is connected to the LAN by a bridge. A remote work-station may be either a stand-alone or part of another network.

restore: To copy data from a backup storage device to the network.

rights: Privileges (assigned by the network supervisor) that control how users may work with files in a given directory (for example, controlling whether a user may read a file, change a file, or delete a file). *Trustee* rights are assigned to individual users, and control each user's right within directories. A *maximum rights mask* is assigned to each individual directory and restricts the rights of all users (except SUPERVISOR) in the directory, overriding the individual trustee rights of a user.

ROM (read-only memory): Permanent memory built into a device; the data in ROM cannot be erased or changed. Data in ROM can be accessed quickly and in any order (random access). *See also* RAM.

root directory: The highest level in a hierarchical directory structure. It is the main directory on a volume; all other directories are subdirectories of the root directory. Network users with sufficient rights may create subdirectories beneath a root directory. The root directory does not have a name; it is implied by the volume name (for example, SYS:, VOL1:, etc.).

scroll: To move the display on a screen or in a window up, down, left, or right.

search drive: A drive letter assigned to a network directory in which the operating system will automatically search for an executable file (or data files accessed by the executable files) if the file is not found in the current (default) directory. A search drive allows a user working in one directory to access an application that is located in another directory.

sectors: Locations in disk storage. Each disk track is divided into several sectors. In disks using the hard sectoring method, the sectors are marked by holes in the disk. In disks using soft sectoring, a single hole and a timing scheme enable the computer to read or write sector boundaries on the disk.

security: The control over users as they access and work with directories and files on a NetWare network. There are four levels of NetWare security: login/password security, trustee security, directory security, and file attributes security. *See also* password protection; rights; file attributes.

security equivalence: A feature of network security that allows the supervisor to quickly and easily assign one user or group the same trustee rights as another user or group.

serial port: A port that allows data to be transmitted one bit at a time. On PC-compatible computers, COM1 and COM2 are asynchronous serial ports.

server: *See* file server.

server console: *See* console.

shell: *See* NetWare shell.

software: The parts of a computer system that are not physical or tangible—usually computer programs.

spool: To transfer data that was intended for a peripheral device (such as a printer) into temporary storage. From there the data can be transferred to the peripheral at a later time, without affecting or delaying the system as it performs other operations.

SPX (Sequenced Packet Exchange): A protocol by which two workstations or applications communicate across the network. SPX uses IPX to deliver the messages, but SPX guarantees delivery of the messages and maintains the order of messages on the packet stream.

station: *See* network station.

station address: A unique number assigned to each station on a network. It may be specified in either decimal or hexidecimal format. Also called "physical node address" or "node address."

station number: *See* connection number.

storage: A device or medium (floppy diskette, hard disk, magnetic tape, etc.) that receives and holds data for retrieval. Storage may be permanent or temporary.

subdirectory: Any directory that is below another directory in the directory structure. For example, SYS:ACCOUNT/RECEIVE is a subdirectory of SYS:ACCOUNT.

supervisor:

1) The *network supervisor* is the person responsible for the smooth operation of the whole network. (The supervisor may also install the network.) The network supervisor maintains the network, reconfiguring and updating it as the need arises.

2) The *user SUPERVISOR* is a special username that is automatically created when a file server is initialized. This user is permanent and cannot be deleted or renamed. The user SUPERVISOR has all rights in all file server volumes and directories, and these rights cannot be revoked. Other users or groups may be granted a security equivalence to the SUPERVISOR.

system console: *See* console.

system hard disk: The first hard disk (internal or external) to be initialized when NetWare is installed on a file server. The system hard disk contains the SYS: volume on which the NetWare utilities are stored.

tape backup unit: *See* disk subsystem.

topology: The physical layout of network components (cable, stations, gateways, hubs, and so on). There are three basic interconnection topologies—star, ring, and bus networks. On a star network, worksta-tions connect directly to a file server but *not* to each other. On a ring net-work, the file server and workstations are cabled in a ring, and a workstation's messages may have to pass through several other worksta-tions before reaching the file server. On a bus network, all workstations and the file server are connected to a central cable (called a trunk or bus).

tracks: Physical locations on a data storage medium. On a disk, tracks take the form of concentric circles. Tracks are divided into sec-tors to form the fundamental units of disk storage.

transmit: To send electronic signals from station to station through a communication medium (coaxial cable, twisted-pair cable, fiber optics, microwave, etc.).

trustee: A user who has been given specific rights to work in a partic-ular directory or subdirectory.

trustee rights: The rights granted to an individual user allowing that user to work in a particular directory or subdirectory. *See also* rights.

user: Any person who attaches to a file server.

utility: A computer program that conveniently performs one or more basic operating system tasks, such as copying files.

volume: A portion of hard disk storage space of predetermined size. A volume is the highest level in a hierarchical directory structure (the same level as a DOS root directory). A hard disk is divided into one or more volumes by the network installer; these volumes can be divided into directories by network users who have the necessary rights.

warm boot: To reload a computer's operating system into memory while the computer is on. Warm boot an IBM PC-compatible computer by simultaneously pressing the Ctrl, Alt, and Del keys. *See also* boot.

wildcard character: A character recognized by a software application as a universal replacement for other characters. NetWare recognizes the * and ? wildcard characters. For example, to copy all files in a directory with filenames that include the extension .EXE, you would type **COPY *.EXE**. The asterisk would represent any combination of characters that precedes the period.

workstation: Any individual personal computer that is connected to a NetWare network and is used to perform tasks (such as word processing) through the use of application programs or utilities.

workstation number: *See* connection number.

write: To record information on a hard disk, floppy diskette, or some other permanent storage device.

Index

M

N

Selections from The SYBEX Library

COMMUNICATIONS

Mastering Crosstalk XVI
Peter W. Gofton
187pp. Ref. 388-0
Recoup the cost of this book in a matter of hours with ready-made routines that speed up and automate your on-line database sessions. Tutorials cover every aspect of installing, running and customizing Crosstalk XVI.

DOS

The ABC's of DOS 4
Alan R. Miller
250pp. Ref. 583-2
This step-by-step introduction to using DOS 4 is written especially for beginners. Filled with simple examples, *The ABC's of DOS 4* covers the basics of hardware, software, disks, the system editor EDLIN, DOS commands, and more.

ABC's of MS-DOS
(Second Edition)
Alan R. Miller
233pp. Ref. 493-3
This handy guide to MS-DOS is all many PC users need to manage their computer files, organize floppy and hard disks, use EDLIN, and keep their computers organized. Additional information is given about utilities like Sidekick, and there is a DOS command and program summary. The second edition is fully updated for Version 3.3.

Mastering DOS
(Second Edition)
Judd Robbins
700pp. Ref. 555-7
"The most useful DOS book." This seven-part, in-depth tutorial addresses the needs of users at all levels. Topics range from running applications, to managing

files and directories, configuring the system, batch file programming, and techniques for system developers.

MS-DOS Handbook
(Third Edition)
Richard Allen King
362pp. Ref. 492-5
This classic has been fully expanded and revised to include the latest features of MS-DOS Version 3.3. Two reference books in one, this title has separate sections for programmer and user. Multi-DOS partitons, 3 1/2disk format, batch file call and return feature, and comprehensive coverage of MS-DOS commands are included.

MS-DOS Power User's Guide,
Volume I
(Second Edition)
Jonathan Kamin
482pp. Ref. 473-9
A fully revised, expanded edition of our best-selling guide to high-performance DOS techniques and utilities--with details on Version 3.3. Configuration, I/O, directory structures, hard disks, RAM disks, batch file programming, the ANSI.SYS device driver, more.

MS-DOS Power User's Guide,
Volume II
Martin Waterhouse/Jonathan Kamin
418pp, Ref. 411-9
A second volume of high-performance techniques and utilities, with expanded coverage of DOS 3.3, and new material on video modes, Token-Ring and PC Network support, micro-mainframe links, extended and expanded memory, multi-tasking systems, and more.

DOS User's Desktop Companion
Judd Robbins
969 pp. Ref. 505-0 Softcover
459-3 Hardcover
This comprehensive reference covers DOS commands, batch files, memory

enhancements, printing, communications and more information on optimizing each user's DOS environment. Written with step-by-step instructions and plenty of examples, this volume covers all versions through 3.3.

MS-DOS Advanced Programming
Michael J. Young
490pp. Ref. 578-6

Practical techniques for maximizing performance in MS-DOS software by making best use of system resources. Topics include functions, interrupts, devices, multitasking, memory residency and more, with examples in C and assembler.

Essential PC-DOS (Second Edition)
Myril Clement Shaw/ Susan Soltis Shaw
332pp. Ref. 413-5

An authoritative guide to PC-DOS, including version 3.2. Designed to make experts out of beginners, it explores everything from disk management to batch file programming. Includes an 85-page command summary.

The IBM PC-DOS Handbook (Third Edition)
Richard Allen King
359pp. Ref. 512-3

A guide to the inner workings of PC-DOS 3.2, for intermediate to advanced users and programmers of the IBM PC series. Topics include disk, screen and port control, batch files, networks, compatibility, and more.

DOS Instant Reference SYBEX Prompter Series
Greg Harvey/Kay Yarborough Nelson
220pp. Ref. 477-1; 4 3/4x8

A complete fingertip reference for fast, easy on-line help:command summaries, syntax, usage and error messages. Organized by function--system commands, file commands, disk management, directories, batch files, I/O, networking, programming, and more.

OTHER OPERATING SYSTEMS AND ENVIRONMENTS

Essential OS/2
Judd Robbins
367pp. Ref. 478-X

This introduction to OS/2 for new and prospective users offers clear explanations of multitasking, details key OS/2 commands and functions, and updates current DOS users to the new OS/2 world. Details are also given for users to run existing DOS programs under OS/2.

Programmer's Guide to OS/2
Michael J. Young
625pp. Ref. 464-X

This concise introduction gives a complete overview of program development under OS/2, with careful attention to new tools and features. Topics include MS-DOS compatibility, device drivers, services, graphics, windows, the LAN manager, and more.

Programmer's Guide to GEM
Phillip Balma/William Fitler
504pp. Ref. 297-3

GEM programming from the ground up, including the Resource Construction Set, ICON Editor, and Virtual Device Interface. Build a complete graphics application with objects, events, menus, windows, alerts and dialogs.

Understanding Hard Disk Management
Jonathan Kamin
500pp. Ref. 561-1

Put your work, your office or your entire business literally at your fingertips, in a customized, automated MS-DOS work environment. Topics include RAM disks, extended and expanded memory, and more.

Programmer's Guide to Windows (Second Edition)
David Durant/Geta Carlson/Paul Yao

704pp. Ref. 496-8

The first edition of this programmer's guide was hailed as a classic. This new edition covers Windows 2 and Windows/386 in depth. Special emphasis is given to over fifty new routines to the Windows interface, and to preparation for OS/2 Presentation Manager compatibility.

Graphics Programming Under Windows
Brian Myers/Chris Doner
646pp. Ref. 448-8

Straightforward discussion, abundant examples, and a concise reference guide to graphics commands make this book a must for Windows programmers. Topics range from how Windows works to programming for business, animation, CAD, and desktop publishing. For Version 2.

HARDWARE

The RS-232 Solution
Joe Campbell
194pp. Ref. 140-3

A complete how-to guide to trouble-free RS-232-C interfacing from scratch. In-depth coverage of concepts, techniques and testing devices, and case studies deriving cables for a variety of common computers, printers and modems.

Mastering Serial Communications
Peter W. Gofton
289pp. Ref. 180-2

The software side of communications, with details on the IBM PC's serial programming, the XMODEM and Kermit protocols, non-ASCII data transfer, interrupt-level programming and more. Sample programs in C, assembly language and BASIC.

Microprocessor Interfacing Techniques (Third Edition)
Austin Lesea/Rodnay Zaks
456pp. Ref. 029-6

This handbook is for engineers and hobbyists alike, covering every aspect of interfacing microprocessors with peripheral devices. Topics include assembling a CPU, basic I/O, analog circuitry, and bus standards.

From Chips to Systems: An Introduction to Microcomputers (Second Edition)
Rodnay Zaks/Alexander Wolfe
580pp. Ref. 377-5

The best-selling introduction to microcomputer hardware--now fully updated, revised, and illustrated. Such recent advances as 32-bit processors and RISC architecture are introduced and explained for the first time in a beginning text.

Mastering Digital Device Control
William G. Houghton
366pp. Ref. 346-5

Complete principles of system design using single-chip microcontrollers, with numerous examples. Topics include expanding memory and I/O, interfacing with multi-chip CPUs, clocks, display devices, analog measurements, and much more.

SPREADSHEETS AND INTEGRATED SOFTWARE

The ABC's of 1-2-3 (Second Edition)
Chris Gilbert/Laurie Williams
245pp. Ref. 355-4

Online Today recommends it as "an easy and comfortable way to get started with the program." An essential tutorial for novices, it will remain on your desk as a valuable source of ongoing reference and support. For Release 2.

Mastering 1-2-3 (Second Edition)
Carolyn Jorgensen
702pp. Ref. 528-X

Get the most from 1-2-3 Release 2 with this step-by-step guide emphasizing advanced features and practical uses.

Topics include data sharing, macros, spreadsheet security, expanded memory, and graphics enhancements.

Lotus 1-2-3 Desktop Companion (SYBEX Ready Reference Series)
Greg Harvey
976pp. Ref. 501-8

A full-time consultant, right on your desk. Hundreds of self-contained entries cover every 1-2-3 feature, organized by topic, indexed and cross-referenced, and supplemented by tips, macros and working examples. For Release 2.

Advanced Techniques in Lotus 1-2-3
Peter Antoniak/E. Michael Lunsford
367pp. Ref. 556-5

This guide for experienced users focuses on advanced functions, and techniques for designing menu-driven applications using macros and the Release 2 command language. Interfacing techniques and add-on products are also considered.

Lotus 1-2-3 Tips and Tricks
Gene Weisskopf
396pp. Ref. 454-2

A rare collection of timesavers and tricks for longtime Lotus users. Topics include macros, range names, spreadsheet design, hardware considerations, DOS operations, efficient data analysis, printing, data interchange, applications development, and more.

Lotus 1-2-3 Instant Reference SYBEX Prompter Series
Greg Harvey/Kay Yarborough Nelson
296pp. Ref. 475-5; 4 3/4x8

Organized information at a glance. When you don't have time to hunt through hundreds of pages of manuals, turn here for a quick reminder: the right key sequence, a brief explanation of a command, or the correct syntax for a specialized function.

Mastering Lotus HAL
Mary V. Campbell
342pp. Ref. 422-4

A complete guide to using HAL "natural language" requests to communicate with 1-2-3—for new and experienced users. Covers all the basics, plus advanced HAL features such as worksheet linking and auditing, macro recording, and more.

Mastering Symphony (Fourth Edition)
Douglas Cobb
857pp. Ref. 494-1

Thoroughly revised to cover all aspects of the major upgrade of Symphony Version 2, this Fourth Edition of Doug Cobb's classic is still "the Symphony bible" to this complex but even more powerful package. All the new features are discussed and placed in context with prior versions so that both new and previous users will benefit from Cobb's insights.

The ABC's of Quattro
Alan Simpson/Douglas J. Wolf
286pp. Ref. 560-3

Especially for users new to spreadsheets, this is an introduction to the basic concepts and a guide to instant productivity through editing and using spreadsheet formulas and functions. Includes how to print out graphs and data for presentation. For Quattro 1.1.

Mastering Quattro
Alan Simpson
576pp. Ref. 514-X

This tutorial covers not only all of Quattro's classic spreadsheet features, but also its added capabilities including extended graphing, modifiable menus, and the macro debugging environment. Simpson brings out how to use all of Quattro's new-generation-spreadsheet capabilities.

Mastering Framework II
Douglas Hergert/Jonathan Kamin
509pp. Ref. 390-2

This business-minded tutorial includes a complete introduction to idea processing, "frames," and software integration, along with its comprehensive treatment of word processing, spreadsheet, and database management with Framework.

The ABC's of Excel
on the IBM PC
Douglas Hergert
326pp. Ref. 567-0

This book is a brisk and friendly introduction to the most important features of Microsoft Excel for PC's. This beginner's book discusses worksheets, charts, database operations, and macros, all with hands-on examples. Written for all versions through Version 2.

Mastering Excel on the IBM PC
Carl Townsend
628pp. Ref. 403-8

A complete Excel handbook with step-by-step tutorials, sample applications and an extensive reference section. Topics include worksheet fundamentals, formulas and windows, graphics, database techniques, special features, macros and more.

Mastering Enable
Keith D. Bishop
517pp. Ref. 440-2

A comprehensive, practical, hands-on guide to Enable 2.0—integrated word processing, spreadsheet, database management, graphics, and communications—from basic concepts to custom menus, macros and the Enable Procedural Language.

Mastering Q & A
(Second Edition)
Greg Harvey
540pp. Ref. 452-6

This hands-on tutorial explores the Q & A Write, File, and Report modules, and the Intelligent Assistant. English-language command processor, macro creation, interfacing with other software, and more, using practical business examples.

Mastering SuperCalc 4
Greg Harvey
311pp. Ref. 419-4

A guided tour of this spreadsheet, database and graphics package shows how and why it adds up to a powerful business planning tool. Step-by-step lessons and real-life examples cover every aspect of the program.

Understanding Javelin PLUS
John R. Levine
Margaret Levine Young
Jordan M. Young
558pp. Ref. 358-9

This detailed guide to Javelin's latest release includes a concise introduction to business modeling, from profit-and-loss analysis to manufacturing studies. Readers build sample models and produce multiple reports and graphs, to master Javelin's unique features.

DATABASE
MANAGEMENT

Mastering Paradox
(Third Edition)
Alan Simpson
663pp. Ref. 490-9

Paradox is given authoritative, comprehensive explanation in Simpson's up-to-date new edition which goes from database basics to command-file programming with PAL. Topics include multiuser networking, the Personal Programmer Application Generator, the Data-Entry Toolkit, and more.

The ABC's of dBASE IV
Robert Cowart
300pp. Ref. 531-X

This superb tutorial introduces beginners to the concept of databases and practical dBASE IV applications featuring the new menu-driven interface, the new report writer, and Query by Example.

Understanding dBASE IV
(Special Edition)
Alan Simpson
880pp. Ref. 509-3

This Special Edition is the best introduction to dBASE IV, written by 1 million-reader-strong dBASE expert Alan Simpson. First it gives basic skills for creating and manipulating efficient databases. Then the author explains how to make reports, manage multiple databases, and build applications. Includes Fast Track speed notes.

dBASE III PLUS Programmer's Reference Guide
(SYBEX Ready Reference Series)
Alan Simpson
1056pp. Ref. 508-5

Programmers will save untold hours and effort using this comprehensive, well-organized dBASE encyclopedia. Complete technical details on commands and functions, plus scores of often-needed algorithms.

The ABC's of dBASE III PLUS
Robert Cowart
264pp. Ref. 379-1

The most efficient way to get beginners up and running with dBASE. Every 'how' and 'why' of database management is demonstrated through tutorials and practical dBASE III PLUS applications.

Mastering dBASE III PLUS:
A Structured Approach
Carl Townsend
342pp. Ref. 372-4

In-depth treatment of structured programming for custom dBASE solutions. An ideal study and reference guide for applications developers, new and experienced users with an interest in efficient programming.

Also:
Mastering dBASE III: A Structured Approach
Carl Townsend
338pp. Ref. 301-5

Understanding dBASE III PLUS
Alan Simpson
415pp. Ref. 349-X

A solid sourcebook of training and ongoing support. Everything from creating a first database to command file programming is presented in working examples, with tips and techniques you won't find anywhere else.

Also:
Understanding dBASE III
Alan Simpson
300pp. Ref. 267-1

Understanding dBASE II
Alan Simpson
260pp. Ref. 147-0

Advanced Techniques in dBASE III PLUS
Alan Simpson
454pp. Ref. 369-4

A full course in database design and structured programming, with routines for inventory control, accounts receivable, system management, and integrated databases.

Simpson's dBASE Tips and Tricks (For dBASE III PLUS)
Alan Simpson
420pp. Ref. 383-X

A unique library of techniques and programs shows how creative use of built-in features can solve all your needs--without expensive add-on products or external languages. Spreadsheet functions, graphics, and much more.

Expert dBASE III PLUS
Judd Robbins/Ken Braly
423pp. Ref. 404-6

Experienced dBASE programmers learn scores of advanced techniques for maximizing performance and efficiency in program design, development and testing, database design, indexing, input and output, using compilers, and much more.

dBASE Instant Reference
SYBEX Prompter Series
Alan Simpson
471pp. Ref. 484-4; 4 3/4x8

Comprehensive information at a glance: a brief explanation of syntax and usage for every dBASE command, with step-by-step instructions and exact keystroke sequences. Commands are grouped by function in twenty precise categories.

Understanding R:BASE
Alan Simpson/Karen Watterson
609pp. Ref.503-4

This is the definitive R:BASE tutorial, for use with either OS/2 or DOS. Hands-on lessons cover every aspect of the software, from creating and using a database, to custom systems. Includes Fast Track speed notes.

Also:
Understanding R:BASE 5000
Alan Simpson
413pp. Ref. 302-3

Understanding Oracle
James T. Perry/Joseph G. Lateer
634pp. Ref. 534-4
A comprehensive guide to the Oracle database management system for administrators, users, and applications developers. Covers everything in Version 5 from database basics to multi-user systems, performance, and development tools including SQL*Forms, SQL*Report, and SQL*Calc. Includes Fast Track speed notes.

WORD PROCESSING

The ABC's of WordPerfect 5
Alan R. Neibauer
283pp. Ref. 504-2
This introduction explains the basics of desktop publishing with WordPerfect 5: editing, layout, formatting, printing, sorting, merging, and more. Readers are shown how to use WordPerfect 5's new features to produce great-looking reports.

The ABC's of WordPerfect
Alan R. Neibauer
239pp. Ref. 425-9
This basic introduction to WordPefect consists of short, step-by-step lessons—for new users who want to get going fast. Topics range from simple editing and formatting, to merging, sorting, macros, and more. Includes version 4.2

Mastering WordPerfect 5
Susan Baake Kelly
709pp. Ref. 500-X
The revised and expanded version of this definitive guide is now on WordPerfect 5 and covers wordprocessing and basic desktop publishing. As more than 200,000 readers of the original edition can attest, no tutorial approaches it for clarity and depth of treatment. Sorting, line drawing, and laser printing included.

Mastering WordPerfect
Susan Baake Kelly
435pp. Ref. 332-5
Step-by-step training from startup to mastery, featuring practical uses (form letters, newsletters and more), plus advanced topics such as document security and macro creation, sorting and columnar math. Includes Version 4.2.

Advanced Techniques in WordPerfect 5
Kay Yarborough Nelson
586pp. Ref. 511-5
Now updated for Version 5, this invaluable guide to the advanced features of Word-Perfect provides step-by-step instructions and practical examples covering those specialized techniques which have most perplexed users--indexing, outlining, foreign-language typing, mathematical functions, and more.

WordPerfect Desktop Companion
SYBEX Ready Reference Series
Greg Harvey/Kay Yarbourough Nelson
663pp. Ref. 507-7
This compact encyclopedia offers detailed, cross-referenced entries on every software feature, organized for fast, convenient on-the-job help. Includes self-contained enrichment material with tips, techniques and macros. Special information is included about laser printing using WordPerfect that is not available elsewhere. For Version 4.2.

WordPerfect 5 Desktop Companion
SYBEX Ready Reference Series
Greg Harvey/Kay Yarborough Nelson
1000pp. Ref. 522-0
Desktop publishing features have been added to this compact encyclopedia. This title offers more detailed, cross-referenced entries on every software features including page formatting and

layout, laser printing and word processing macros. New users of WordPerfect, and those new to Version 5 and desktop publishing will find this easy to use for on-the-job help. For Version 5.

WordPerfect Tips and Tricks (Third Edition)
Alan R. Neibauer
650pp. Ref. 520-4

This new edition is a real timesaver. For on-the-job guidance and creative new uses, this title covers all versions of Word-Perfect up to and including 5.0—covers streamlining documents, automating with macros, new print enhancements, and more.

WordPerfect 5 Instant Reference
Greg Harvey/Kay Yarborough Nelson
316pp. Ref. 535-2

This pocket-sized reference has all the program commands for the powerful WordPerfect 5 organized alphabetically for quick access. Each command entry has the exact key sequence, any reveal codes, a list of available options, and option-by-option discussions.

WordPerfect Instant Reference SYBEX Prompter Series
Greg Harvey/Kay Yarborough Nelson
254pp. Ref. 476-3

When you don't have time to go digging through the manuals, this fingertip guide offers clear, concise answers: command summaries, correct usage, and exact keystroke sequences for on-the-job tasks. Convenient organization reflects the structure of WordPerfect.

Mastering SAMNA
Ann McFarland Draper
503pp. Ref. 376-7

Word-processing professionals learn not just how, but also when and why to use SAMNA's many powerful features. Master the basics, gain power-user skills, return again and again for reference and expert tips.

The ABC's of Microsoft WORD
Alan R. Neibauer
321pp. Ref. 497-6

Users who want to wordprocess straightforward documents and print elegant reports without wading through reams of documentation will find all they need to know about MicroSoft WORD in this basic guide. Simple editing, formatting, merging, sorting, macros and style sheets are detailed.

Mastering Microsoft WORD (Third Edition)
Matthew Holtz
638pp. Ref. 524-7

This comprehensive, step-by-step guide includes Version 4.0. Hands-on tutorials treat everything from word processing basics to the fundamentals of desktop publishing, stressing business applications throughout.

Advanced Techinques in Microsoft WORD
Alan R. Neibauer
537pp. Ref. 416-X

The book starts with a brief overview, but the main focus is on practical applications using advanced features. Topics include customization, forms, style sheets, columns, tables, financial documents, graphics and data management.

Mastering DisplayWrite 4
Michael E. McCarthy
447pp. Ref. 510-7

Total training, reference and support for users at all levels--in plain, non-technical language. Novices will be up and running in an hour's time; everyone will gain complete word-processing and document-management skills.

Mastering MultiMate Advantage II
Charles Ackerman
407pp. Ref. 482-8

This comprehensive tutorial covers all the capabilities of MultiMate, and highlights the differences between MultiMate Advantage II and previous versions--in pathway support, sorting, math, DOS access, using dBASE III, and more. With many practical examples, and a chapter on the On-File database.

The Complete Guide to MultiMate
Carol Holcomb Dreger
208pp. Ref. 229-9

This step-by-step tutorial is also an excellent reference guide to MultiMate features and uses. Topics include search/replace, library and merge functions, repagination, document defaults and more.

Advanced Techniques in MultiMate
Chris Gilbert
275pp. Ref. 412-7

A textbook on efficient use of MultiMate for business applications, in a series of self-contained lessons on such topics as multiple columns, high-speed merging, mailing-list printing and Key Procedures.

Introduction to WordStar
Arthur Naiman
208pp. Ref. 134-9

This all time bestseller is an engaging first-time introduction to word processing as well as a complete guide to using WordStar--from basic editing to blocks, global searches, formatting, dot commands, SpellStar and MailMerge.

Mastering Wordstar on the IBM PC (Second Edition)
Arthur Naiman
200pp. Ref. 392-9

A specially revised and expanded introduction to Wordstar with SpellStar and MailMerge. Reviewers call it "clearly written, conveniently organized, generously illustrated and definitely designed from the user's point of view."

Practical WordStar Uses
Julie Anne Arca
303pp. Ref. 107-1

A hands-on guide to WordStar and MailMerge applications, with solutions to comon problems and "recipes" for day-to-day tasks. Formatting, merge-printing and much more; plus a quick-reference command chart and notes on CP/M and PC-DOS.

Practical Techniques in WordStar Release 4
Julie Anne Arca
334pp. Ref. 465-8

A task oriented approach to WordStar Release 4 and the DOS operating system. Special applications are covered in detail with summaries of important commands and step-by-step instructions.

Mastering WordStar Release 4
Greg Harvey
413pp. Ref. 399-6

Practical training and reference for the latest WordStar release--from startup to advanced featues. Experienced users will find new features highlighted and illustrated with hands-on examples. Covers math, macros, laser printers and more.

WordStar Instant Reference
David J. Clark
314pp. Ref. 543-3

This quick reference provides reminders on the use of the editing, formatting, mailmerge, and document processing commands available through WordStar 4 and 5. Operations are organized alphabetically for easy access. The text includes a survey of the menu system and instructions for installing and customizing WordStar.

TO JOIN THE SYBEX MAILING LIST OR ORDER BOOKS
PLEASE COMPLETE THIS FORM

NAME _____ COMPANY _____

STREET _____ CITY _____

STATE _____ ZIP _____

☐ PLEASE MAIL ME MORE INFORMATION ABOUT **SYBEX** TITLES

ORDER FORM (There is no obligation to order)

PLEASE SEND ME THE FOLLOWING:

TITLE	QTY	PRICE
_____	____	____
_____	____	____
_____	____	____
_____	____	____

TOTAL BOOK ORDER   ____ $____

CUSTOMER SIGNATURE _____

SHIPPING AND HANDLING PLEASE ADD $2.00
PER BOOK VIA UPS   ____

FOR OVERSEAS SURFACE ADD $5.25 PER
BOOK PLUS $4.40 REGISTRATION FEE   ____

FOR OVERSEAS AIRMAIL ADD $18.25 PER
BOOK PLUS $4.40 REGISTRATION FEE   ____

CALIFORNIA RESIDENTS PLEASE ADD
APPLICABLE SALES TAX   ____

TOTAL AMOUNT PAYABLE   ____

☐ CHECK ENCLOSED   ☐ VISA
☐ MASTERCARD   ☐ AMERICAN EXPRESS

ACCOUNT NUMBER _____

EXPIR. DATE _____ DAYTIME PHONE _____

CHECK AREA OF COMPUTER INTEREST:

☐ BUSINESS SOFTWARE

☐ TECHNICAL PROGRAMMING

☐ OTHER: _____

THE FACTOR THAT WAS MOST IMPORTANT IN YOUR SELECTION:

☐ THE SYBEX NAME

☐ QUALITY

☐ PRICE

☐ EXTRA FEATURES

☐ COMPREHENSIVENESS

☐ CLEAR WRITING

☐ OTHER _____

OTHER COMPUTER TITLES YOU WOULD LIKE TO SEE IN PRINT:

_____

_____

OCCUPATION

☐ PROGRAMMER   ☐ TEACHER

☐ SENIOR EXECUTIVE   ☐ HOMEMAKER

☐ COMPUTER CONSULTANT   ☐ RETIRED

☐ SUPERVISOR   ☐ STUDENT

☐ MIDDLE MANAGEMENT   ☐ OTHER:

☐ ENGINEER/TECHNICAL   _____

☐ CLERICAL/SERVICE

☐ BUSINESS OWNER/SELF EMPLOYED

CHECK YOUR LEVEL OF COMPUTER USE

☐ NEW TO COMPUTERS

☐ INFREQUENT COMPUTER USER

☐ FREQUENT USER OF ONE SOFTWARE

    PACKAGE:

    NAME _____

☐ FREQUENT USER OF MANY SOFTWARE

    PACKAGES

☐ PROFESSIONAL PROGRAMMER

OTHER COMMENTS:

_____

_____

_____

_____

_____

_____

_____

PLEASE FOLD, SEAL, AND MAIL TO SYBEX

SYBEX, INC.
2021 CHALLENGER DR. #100
ALAMEDA, CALIFORNIA USA
           94501

SEAL

SYBEX Computer Books are different.

Here is why . . .

At SYBEX, each book is designed with you in mind. Every manuscript is carefully selected and supervised by our editors, who are themselves computer experts. We publish the best authors, whose technical expertise is matched by an ability to write clearly and to communicate effectively. Programs are thoroughly tested for accuracy by our technical staff. Our computerized production department goes to great lengths to make sure that each book is well-designed.

In the pursuit of timeliness, SYBEX has achieved many publishing firsts. SYBEX was among the first to integrate personal computers used by authors and staff into the publishing process. SYBEX was the first to publish books on the CP/M operating system, microprocessor interfacing techniques, word processing, and many more topics.

Expertise in computers and dedication to the highest quality product have made SYBEX a world leader in computer book publishing. Translated into fourteen languages, SYBEX books have helped millions of people around the world to get the most from their computers. We hope we have helped you, too.

For a complete catalog of our publications:

SYBEX, Inc. 2021 Challenger Drive, #100, Alameda, CA 94501
Tel: (415) 523-8233/(800) 227-2346   Telex: 336311
Fax: (415) 523-2373

PRINT JOB CONFIGURATION OPTIONS—LISTED ALPHABETICALLY (Cont.)

Option	Description	NetWare Command
NoFormFeed	Turns off end-of-job form feed at the printer. Saves a sheet of blank paper at the end of a print job.	CAPTURE and NPRINT
NoTabs	Cancels all tab and control character interpretations by the queue print formatter (i.e. prints the job "as is," with the special codes the application embedded in the document).	CAPTURE and NPRINT
Queue = *queue*	Indicates which queue a print job is sent to. *queue* is the print queue name.	CAPTURE and NPRINT
Server = *servername*	Indicates which file server the data should be sent to, if other than your default.	CAPTURE and NPRINT
SHow	Displays current CAPTURE settings. May not be used with any other CAPTURE option.	CAPTURE
Tabs = *n*	Replaces tabs in a document with the number of spaces you specify (*n*). Used only when an application does not have a print formatter. You can specify up to 18 spaces per tab.	CAPTURE and NPRINT
TImeout = *n*	The time (*n*), in seconds (from 1 to 1000), between pressing an application's print keys and when the print job is sent to the file server. The default is 0.	CAPTURE

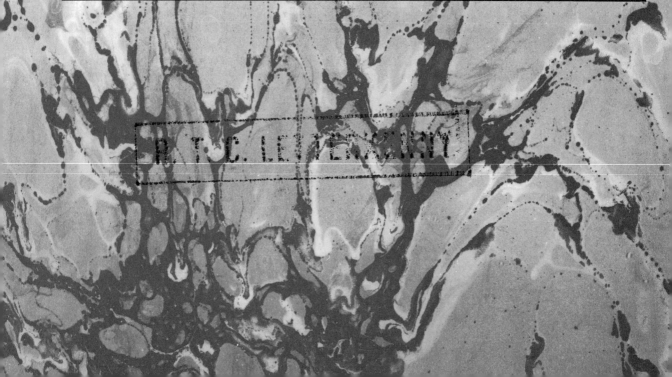